Driving

—— THE ——
DEVELOPMENT AND USE OF
HORSE-DRAWN VEHICLES

Driving

THE
DEVELOPMENT AND USE OF
HORSE-DRAWN VEHICLES

Clive Richardson

B.T. Batsford Ltd London

© Clive Richardson 1985
First published 1985

All rights reserved. No part of this publication
may be reproduced, in any form or by any means,
without permission from the Publisher

ISBN 0 7134 3992 0

Typeset by Servis Filmsetting Ltd, Manchester
and printed in Great Britain by
Butler & Tanner Ltd, Frome and London

for the publishers
B.T. Batsford Ltd
4 Fitzhardinge Street
London W1H 0AH

Line drawings © Clive Richardson and Susan Millard 1985

Contents

List of plates 6
Foreword by HRH *The Duke of Edinburgh* KG, KT 9

1 Early origins 11
2 The first coach 20
3 The golden age 32
4 Behind the scenes 40
5 The private carriage 51
6 Public transport 60
7 Trade vehicles 66
8 Dangerous travel 76
9 In decline 84
10 Revival and its problems 91
11 Competitive driving 109
12 New technology 125
13 Miscellany 134
14 Future prospects 140

Glossary 145
Suppliers and craft firms 147
Carriage museums and collections 149
Select bibliography 151
Index 153

Plates

Between pp. 48 and 49

1 Egyptian chariot, *circa* 1400 BC (Science Museum).
2 Two-wheeled cart with studded wheels, an illustration from the Lutrell psalter, *circa* 1338 (Science Museum).
3 The original brougham, *circa* 1838 (Science Museum).
4 Royal Mail coach, *circa* 1820 (Science Museum).
5 American concord coach, *circa* 1875 (Shelburne Museum).
6 Skeleton brake (Science Museum).
7 Irish jaunting car (Science Museum).
8 American cabriolet sleigh built by The French Carriage Co., Boston, Mass., *circa* 1890 (Shelburne Museum).
9 South African cape cart (Don Triton).
10 Wheelwrights at work hooping wheels, *circa* 1900 (Beamish Hall Museum).
11 Primitive hearse used in rural areas in the North of England until comparatively recently (Beamish Hall Museum).
12 Grantham Dairy Company's prize-winning milk float, *circa* 1900 (Grantham Library).
13 Hansom cab built by Wilkinson of Liverpool, *circa* 1890 (Bath Carriage Museum).
14 American grocer's delivery sleigh (Shelburne Museum).
15 Sefton landau built by Holland and Holland of London (Bath Carriage Museum).
16 Four-wheeled dogcart built by Thompsons of Perth, Scotland (Bath Carriage Museum).
17 Sociable, built by Silk and Son of London (Bath Carriage Museum).
18 Carrier's wagon, *circa* 1900 (Beamish Hall Museum).
19 Oil delivery tanker, *circa* 1900 (Beamish Hall Museum).
20 Pair horse wagonette, *circa* 1910 (Beamish Hall Museum).
21 Three-horse charabanc, *circa* 1900 (Beamish Hall Museum).
22 Horse-drawn tram photographed in the north of England in 1905 (Beamish Hall Museum).

23 Mrs J. DuBois driving a pair of Morgan horse mares to a salon trap built by Flandrau & Co., New York (Phaneuf/Gurdziel).
24 Scaling muck from a coup cart, *circa* 1910 (Beamish Hall Museum).
25 Furniture removal van, *circa* 1910 (Beamish Hall Museum).
26 Clarence, built by the Gloucester Wagon Works (Bath Carriage Museum).
27 Whip behind! (Beamish Hall Museum).
28 Harvest carts in the north of England, *circa* 1920 (Beamish Hall Museum).
29 Mrs Anne Ashworth driving a Morgan horse stallion to an American road cart (Phaneuf/Gurdziel).
30 John Coxon, coachman to a Co. Durham doctor, waits outside a patient's house with the horse and gig while his employer makes a visit. *Circa* 1912. (Beamish Hall Museum)
31 A smart Hackney driven to a butcher's boxcart in a trade turnout class (Ken Ettridge).
Between pp. 80 and 81
32 Mr Peter DuBois driving a Morgan horse stallion to a Meadowbrook built by French & Co. of Boston, Mass. (Phaneuf/Gurdziel).
33 Horse-drawn tanker, *circa* 1900 (Beamish Hall Museum).
34 Phaeton built by Cund & Co. of Stourbridge (Bath Carriage Museum).
35 Miss S. Smith driving her pair of Hackney ponies to a modern equirotal phaeton during the marathon phase of a combined driving event (Ken Ettridge).
36 Mr E. Dickinson's pair of Dales pony mares driven to a four-wheeled trade lorry in a trade turnout class (Ken Ettridge).
37 Mr A. Holder's team at the end of the marathon phase of a combined driving event (Ken Ettridge).
38 Mrs W. Skill's Hackney driven to a Liverpool gig in a private driving class (Ken Ettridge).
39 American milk wagon built by the Parsons Wagon Co., New York, *circa* 1900 (Shelburne Museum).
40 The author driving a Morgan horse gelding to a Meadowbrook during the presentation phase of a combined driving event (Ken Ettridge).
41 Basket *vis-à-vis* phaeton (Bath Carriage Museum).
42 A competitor negotiates a steep hill during the marathon phase of a combined driving event (Sandra Caton).
43 Mr George Bowman driving his team through the watersplash on the marathon phase of a combined driving event (Ken Ettridge).

44 Miss Sylvia Brocklebank driving her grey Hackney Optimistic to a viceroy, winner of the open harness class at Grantham Show in 1913 (Grantham Library).

45 Miss Claudia Bunn driving a tandem of Welsh ponies to a two-wheeled competition vehicle during the obstacle driving phase of a combined driving event (Ken Ettridge).

46 A competitor in trouble on the marathon of a combined driving event (Ken Ettridge).

47 Mr George Bowman driving his team of Lippizaners to a modern competition vehicle (Ken Ettridge).

48 Brougham, built by Tucker & Co. of London (Bath Carriage Museum).

49 Mr Emil Jung driving a team of Holsteiners to a modern Daresbury phaeton (Ken Ettridge).

50 Horse omnibus, *circa* 1880 (Science Museum).

51 Mr Keith Farnhill driving his team to a modern Presteigne dogcart (Ken Ettridge).

52 Mr W. Moorhouse driving a Welsh pony to a ralli car in a private driving class (Ken Ettridge).

53 Wagonette built by Hooper of London (Bath Carriage Museum).

54 Mr Mark Broadbent driving a team of Welsh ponies to a modern Fenix competition vehicle (Ken Ettridge).

55 HRH The Duke of Edinburgh receiving the winner's trophy at a combined driving event. The vehicle is a modern Bennington phaeton (Ken Ettridge).

56 The perils of combined driving.

57 Australian pony jinker.

58 Mrs D. McDonald driving a pair of Australian ponies to a Whitechapel buggy.

59 Australian sydney sulky (Jo Kirkwood).

Foreword by
HRH *The Duke of Edinburgh* KG, KT

Before the invention of mechanically propelled vehicles little over a century ago, human transport depended on horse and ox power. It was the only practical and economic option. No wonder that when machines became available the use of horses declined, although it never entirely ceased. Amateur coaching became a leisure occupation but considering the cost it was never likely to become widely popular.

Then came the Second World War and petrol rationing, and in no time carts that had been tucked away in barns were brought out and dusted off and the family pony pressed into service. Without this experience gained by so many drivers during the war years, it is doubtful whether the subsequent revival of driving could have developed at the speed it did.

Last on the scene was competitive driving as a sport. Encouraged by rules developed by the International Equestrian Federation in 1969, based on the ridden three-day event, it has now taken its place as one of the major international equestrian sports.

In retrospect it is possible to see that the post-war revival in driving and the development of driving as a sport came just in time. In another few years the experience and traditions of driving could well have died out and the vehicles gone for scrap. As it was, there were just sufficient professionals and experts available to ensure that the new generation of drivers learnt the basic rules of safety, correct harnessing and the care of carriage horses.

The revival in driving also sparked off a revival in literature on the subject, of which this book is an excellent example. The author has taken the story from the earliest beginnings right up to the situation in the present day, and while it will certainly interest contemporary drivers, I have no doubt that it will become a textbook for future generations as well.

Chapter 1
Early origins

No one knows who invented the carriage, or when, but inventions are generally the product of specific needs, and primitive man could carry on his back what few possessions he needed for his nomadic lifestyle. Thus it was not until the neolithic period, when man began living in semi-permanent communities and cultivating the ground with the aid of simple stone tools, that the need for a means of transporting animals killed for food, harvested crops or firewood to a home base was felt. The bough of a tree, upon which the load could be placed and dragged easily over grass or snow, constituted the first primitive sledge, although later examples were crudely constructed from the whole skin of a large animal like a bear. From such humble origins evolved the true sledge, a specifically constructed vehicle of woven saplings or wood, sometimes leather-covered, and the forerunner of what would eventually become the carriage body.

As the domestication of animals suitable for draught purposes became more widespread, the drag sledge was adapted for pulling by an animal. Primitive methods of harnessing left much to be desired, but man soon realized that if the animal was attached to the sledge by ropes only, there would be nothing to prevent the sledge from running forward into the animal's legs when going downhill, so he replaced the ropes with poles, and the idea of shafts was born. The poles were attached to either side of the draught animal, at one end, and dragged along the ground at the other, with the load carried on a platform between the poles. The North American Indians used this form of transport, the travois, to move their tepees from place to place, the shafts acting as support poles when the tepee was erected. A similar vehicle known as the slide car was used in many parts of Europe and Asia until quite recent times. In rural Ireland it was used for carrying peat, the load being stacked in a wicker basket slung between the poles, and during the First World War the slide car was used to transport the wounded at first-aid stations along the Balkan front.

It is believed that the rotating action of a wheel was suggested by the use of rolling logs which were placed under a load in order to move it across the ground. This was almost certainly the method used by the Druids to transport the stones used to mark out their ritual or burial sites like

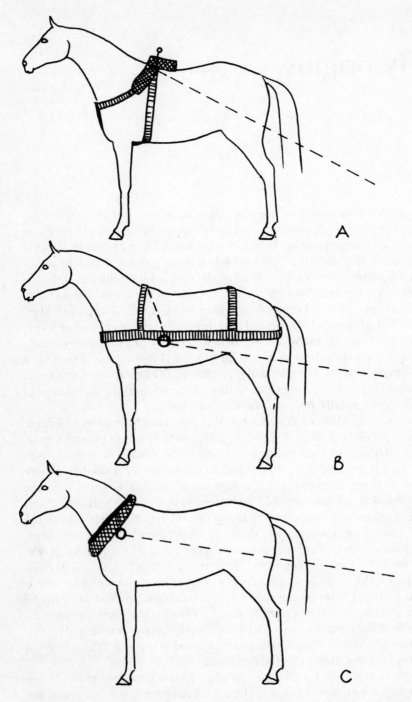

Figure 1 Evolution of harness: *A* throat and girth harness, *B* medieval breast-strap harness, *C* modern collar harness.

Stonehenge in Wiltshire. The realization that, although the larger the roller the easier it was to move the load, very large rollers were too heavy and unwieldy to be practical, and the discovery that it was not essential for the roller to be in contact with the ground for its full length, were major steps forward. By cutting away the middle section of the roller to leave only the central core, the rudimentary shape of a pair of wheels and axle will, at least in theory, have been formed. It is significant that the discovery and initial development of the wheel could only have come at a time when the use of tools for cutting and shaping wood was well established.

The first true wheels were undoubtedly cut from a solid piece of wood, rather like thick slices from a cucumber, with the roughly hewn axle passing through a hole in the centre of the wheel and secured by means of a wedge or pin. The axle revolved with the wheels. The great disadvantage of the solid one-piece wheel was that it tended to split as soon as it was subjected to any stress. Attempts to solve this problem, either by cutting the wheels thicker from the trunk or by strengthening them with the addition of crossbars, effected only a partial remedy and it is most likely that the use of crossbars stemmed from attempts to patch up broken wheels in the first place. Indirectly, these clumsy repair jobs led to a major discovery: the tripartite wheel, which was built of three quite separate pieces of plank cut lengthways and held together with crossbars. Tripartite wheels were considerably stronger than their solid predecessors and they had the advantage of not having to be discarded in the event of a breakage – instead, the broken section of wood could be removed and replaced.

The first cart bodies were very simple in design: usually just a flat platform of planks or wicker, sometimes with low sides to prevent the load from falling out. The rounded axle was kept in place under the body by two pairs of thole pins which formed guides like the rowlocks on a rowing boat, and the axle was positioned in the middle of the body so as to obtain reasonable balance. The most obvious disadvantages of these early vehicles were that, as there were no roads, they could only be used over fairly smooth terrain, and because of the design of the undercarriage they ran best in a straight line. Turning caused problems because the outer wheel was obliged to follow a longer track than the inner wheel and, as both wheels were fixed rigidly to the axle, this caused tremendous friction. Changing direction was also extremely hard work for the animal pulling the vehicle. The invention of wheels that revolved independently on the axle solved the problem and in doing so afforded the early wheelwrights further scope for improvements.

Up until this point axles had been cut square at each end to correspond with the square hole cut out of the centre of each wheel, ensuring a tight and immovable fit. The constant friction caused by the axle turning between the thole pins under the carriage body soon wore through the hardest of woods, despite the use of animal fats as lubrication. It was not a difficult job to shape the axle trees (the parts of the axle which actually passed through the wheels; so named because they were originally always wooden) to a conical shape and to cut circular holes in the wheels themselves so that they could revolve freely on the axle. A pin was again used to keep the wheels in place. With the axle secured to the underside of the vehicle body, the friction was now transferred to the axle trees. Despite the liberal use of lubricants, the centre holes in the wheels still wore very quickly, with the result that the wheels became loose and unsafe. Using softer wood for the axles in the hope that they would take the wear and could then be replaced more easily than a new wheel section proved unsuccessful, as axle strength was sacrificed. The answer was to cover the axle tree with leather that was shrunk on when wet, allowed to dry out completely and well greased with animal fat. Although this could only be a temporary measure, it gave good wear for a reasonable length of time and the leather could be renewed periodically with little trouble. In order to minimize the wear at the rims of the wheels, strips of wood or leather were attached in the form of crude tyres and these, again, were easily renewed from time to time. Leather tyres studded with copper nails were used in Sumeria in the third millennium BC and metal tyres were found in the royal tombs at Ur, *circa* 3000 BC. From the evidence of wheel ruts in the streets of Pompeii, we know that the Romans used metal tyres too.

It is difficult to determine exactly when the spoked wheel came into being, but it was an invention of considerable importance. It came about as a consequence of the early wheelwrights' attempts to produce a wheel that was lighter than the solid type without losing any of the necessary strength, and it must have taken a long time to perfect the technique. The discovery of bronze nave bands for chariot wheels in northern England suggests that the spoked wheel may have been in use in Britain in the late Bronze Age. Unlike the solid or tripartite wheel, the spoked wheel had a certain degree of 'give' or flexibility and was less likely to break in the event of a hard knock or with the strain of being hauled through heavy mud or clay.

The Celts who migrated across Europe from their homelands in the Upper Rhine region were a most important ethnic group, for they were the most skilled cartwrights of ancient times and they brought their skills with them to Britain. It was the Celts who developed the war chariot that was to play such an important role in British warfare. These light two-wheeled vehicles were built of wood, leather or wickerwork, and were designed to be drawn by a pair of ponies. The wheel hubs were made from elm or pine and protruded out from the wheel as much as fifteen inches. The spokes, which were set into the hub, varied in number between ten and fourteen; they were usually pine or hornbeam and turned on a simple lathe to give uniformity. The felloes or wheel rims were bent ash held in place with a metal rim, and the pole on the front of the vehicle was often holly, as this wood is fairly flexible. Occasionally, the wheel hubs were made of oak.

The first accurate description we have of these chariots was written by Julius Caesar, who visited Britain in 55 BC and later wrote that he was not greatly impressed by either the island or its inhabitants, but his description of the *essedum* or war chariot is most interesting. It differed from the Roman chariot in being open at the front rather than at the back, and the wheels had long scythes fixed to the axle trees so that when the chariot was driven at speed through enemy lines the effect was devastating.

Another Roman, Cicero, was also evidently impressed by the Celtic chariots, for he wrote to a friend telling him that there was very little of any value to take away from Britain except the chariots, and that he wished to take one home for his friend as a pattern. The Romans copied many of the Celtic vehicles and even adopted some of the Celtic names for vehicles. Yet another Roman, Tacitus, mentioned that the wives of the British charioteers watched the battles from carts positioned at the edge of the battlefield. This seems to indicate that the wives had travelled to the battlefield in the carts, and this, together with the use of war chariots, represents the first regular use of wheeled vehicles actually for carrying people.

The Roman occupation of western Europe was a significant period in the history of the carriage, for although the Romans were not very skilled in the art of building vehicles, preferring to rely on the talents of those they had conquered, they introduced the important technique of road building. They had learnt the principles of road building from the Etruscans and used it with good effect to make their home city of Rome the centre of a network of connecting roads. In western Europe, the only roads were muddy and rutted tracks between villages which became impassable in winter, and the Romans soon saw the need for good roads so that the quick movement of troops could be carried out. This was imperative if military supremacy was to be maintained, and the first roads, built by involuntary local labour under supervision, connected the Roman camps and fortifications. They were specially built for marching infantry and were paved with stone slabs. This really made them unsuitable for wheeled vehicles, which require a smooth continuous surface. Even so, a number of posting stations were sited along the main highways, with light chariots and post horses kept at the ready for the use of those on official business. A number of resting places offering refreshment or accommodation were also found on many of the major roads – not unlike the coaching inns of later times.

When the Romans were recalled to their besieged capital at the beginning of the fifth century they left a series of sound roads, but it is an indication of the general lack of demand for such roads that they were allowed to fall into disrepair so quickly. A few two-wheeled carts carrying corn, timber or wood still used sections of the roads where and when it was convenient, but they were in the minority. In addition, the lack of trained road technicians aggravated the problem, and those individuals who tried to maintain parts of the roads near villages or settlements generally confined their activities to filling in the potholes on the surface with small stones or earth. Consequently, the repaired sections became stretches of mud in winter or after periods of wet weather, while in summer the earth dried out and blew away in clouds of dust. The example of the Romans was not wasted, however, for they had set a precedent which road builders in later times could copy when the demand for roads again presented itself as a result of the increased volume of traffic.

The Celtic war chariot survived in Britain to a later date than in other European countries, but by the early Middle Ages it was rarely used, although four-wheeled wagons, which many historians believe evolved directly from the sledge with wheels attached rather than as an offshoot of the two-wheeled cart, were becoming more numerous with the invention of the pivoting front axle. Both the Greeks and Romans had tried four-wheeled chariots but found them unsuccessful. The wheelwright was a key figure in the community as his trade was regarded with esteem. Most wheelwrights began their working lives as carpenters and then progressed to specialized work like the construction of vehicle bodies before becoming fully fledged wheelwrights. The old English saying, 'a bad wheelwright makes a good carpenter', is a reminder of the importance of the wheelwright in medieval society. Each vehicle was built individually for a specific demand, and this explains why in illuminated manuscripts and old woodcuts the vehicles pictured differ considerably. The most skilled part of the trade was still the construction of wheels, although by this time one or two improvements were beginning to creep in. One of these was the use of studded or ridged iron tyres which were intended to give the cart a better grip on slippery ground. Ironically, these studs did little to help the abominable state of the roads, and as commerce began to prosper and more vehicles used the roads this became a problem of increasing seriousness. Another innovation was the introduction of wagons covered with awnings of waterproofed cloth to protect the goods or people inside. At first the cover was spread over a wicker frame and secured with ropes, but in later times bent rods in the form of hoops replaced the wicker and horizontal laths were used for strengthening.

A greater variety of carts began to appear on the roads, including vehicles specially designed to carry barrels, logs, sacks of grain, and also people, although there was still a general disdain for riding in a cart which could be traced back to reasons other than just the lack of comfort. One was the idea probably introduced by the Romans that to ride in a vehicle instead of on a horse was a sign of weakness, enervation or decadence. The other was that condemned persons including criminals, murderers and witches, were taken to the scaffold in a tumbril or two-wheeled cart and people did not like the associations.

On fairly good roads and with no interruptions caused either by foot thieves, the forerunners of the highwaymen of coaching days, or sticking fast in potholes and ruts, the average speed for a loaded cart was still disappointingly slow – rarely more than fifteen miles in a day. In readiness for the possibility of getting stuck in the mud or tipping over, wagon and cart drivers frequently carried with them lengths of rope and long poles to use as levers with which to extricate the vehicle. Despite the inherent dangers, many traders still preferred road transport to water transport, which had to contend with the problems of floods and droughts.

The Normans were responsible for introducing a completely new type of vehicle, the horse litter, which quickly gained popularity and was still in use several centuries later. The lightweight covered body was supported by two long poles which ran along each side and projected front and back to form two sets of shafts. These distinctive vehicles, which were originally designed to be carried by footmen, became popular because the comfort of the passengers was not governed by the state of the roads, an important consideration when the roads were in such a deplorable condition. When Margaret, daughter of Henry VII, visited Scotland, she rode for most of the way but when she entered a town she travelled in a litter instead as it was thought a more suitable means of transport for someone in her position. The litter was, however, only used by people of importance or on state occasions, the common people having to use the utilitarian four-wheeled travelling wagon on the few occasions when they did travel by vehicle. The medieval travelling wagon was heavy and slow with only a canvas tarpaulin or leather curtains to protect the passengers, and it was drawn by a pair of horses. Swingletrees, or pivoting wooden bars bolted to the front of the vehicle and having hooks at each end to take the traces, began to appear on many of the wagons and these made the job of actually pulling the vehicles easier for the horses.

Apart from the introduction of the horse litter and one or two minor improvements to the usual pattern of vehicles, the period from the eleventh to the fifteenth century was not, as far as the carriage went, a time of great progress. This was because in a struggling society there was little time or means to foster inventiveness, and also because the bad state of the roads dictated that only the most robust broad-wheeled wagons could be used with any degree of success, so there was little scope for other types of vehicles until something was done about the roads.

In fact no national road maintenance schemes were in operation and the roads gradually grew worse and worse until the thirteenth century, when the first tentative steps were taken to try and ameliorate the situation. Many of even the major roads between European capitals were nothing more than deep-rutted mires with a narrow firm strip running down the centre. If two wagons met face-on, there was inevitably an argument as to which one should move out of the way and risk sinking in the mud or even tipping over. In Britain, a law enacted in 1285 provided for the widening of the roads of many large market towns and also stipulated that even outside the town perimeter all bushes and ditches were to be pulled out or filled in to a distance of two hundred feet on either side of the road. This was to remove any possible cover for footpads as well as providing more room for the vehicles themselves. The Winchester Statutes of the same year decreed that the roads had to be broad enough to allow two vehicles to pass, and the use of studded wheel rims was prohibited. However, with no system to enforce these statutes they had no lasting effect and the roads were soon as bad as before. In some areas road repair and maintenance was undertaken by some of the richer monasteries, who also offered hospitality to the many pilgrims who used the roads journeying to and from the many shrines scattered around Europe.

Although toll roads were a later introduction, during the Middle Ages a few toll bridges were in use. The toll keeper was responsible for the maintenance and upkeep of the bridge and he in turn levied a charge on all travellers using his bridge. Those not wishing to incur the expense either were obliged to risk fording the river which, if the water was high, could be very dangerous with a loaded wagon, or had to turn back and find another, toll-free bridge.

In response to the endless battery of complaints from disgruntled road users, in 1555 the English government made its first serious attempt to instigate a national system of road maintenance. It was called the Highways Act and it remained the basis of administration for nearly three hundred years. This act made the maintenance of roads the responsibility of the local authorities, although it was in fact the parish councils who were called upon to do the work. Each householder was required either to provide the labour for road repairs or to pay a small sum of money instead. Most opted for providing the labour, as they could not afford the cash, but this caused problems as these reluctant workers had little skill and the quality of their workmanship left much to be desired. The inhabitants of one Yorkshire parish expressed in the parish records a disinclination to maintain a stretch of road for the benefit of 'disagreeable strangers'. A surveyor of the highways was appointed in each parish and during his twelve-month term of office he had to inspect the work of his fellow citizens and make reports to the justices of the Highways Sessions. Rather than incur the wrath of their neighbours, most surveyors were prepared to turn a blind eye to almost anything and few cases of unsatisfactory work were reported. While in office, surveyors were generally very unpopular among the people, and they received no remuneration for their thankless task. As surveyors had little incentive to be conscientious in their work and because the Act was not properly enforced, its effectiveness was limited. Only nineteen years before the Act was passed, the dissolution of the monasteries on Henry VIII's directive had presented ransackers with problems when they could not cart the lead from the roofs away 'tille next summer, for the ways are so foule and deepe that no carriage can pass in winter'. William Harrison, the author of *An Elizabethan Guide to England*, 1658, described the roads as 'verie deepe and troublesome in the winter halfe'. It is recorded that even in summer a heavy rainstorm was sufficient to turn the roads into such a mire that as many as ten horses were needed to draw a heavily loaded wagon.

With goods traffic becoming a permanent feature of the summer roads, the first public passenger vehicles came into regular use at the end of the fifteenth century. The stage wagon was the predecessor of all public vehicles; it was slow, averaging two miles an hour, and very uncomfortable as it was unsprung (although suspended bodies were being experimented with on the Continent), but it was inexpensive and within the means of ordinary people. Drawn by teams of four, six or even eight horses, stage or long wagons could seat up to twenty persons plus their baggage, and they were driven by a wagoner, either mounted on a handy cob or on foot, whose job it was to keep the horses moving by means of a long whip. Owing to the speed at which they creaked and groaned along, these vehicles were colloquially known as the 'snails of the highway'. The name *stage* wagon came from the system of changing horses at regular stages along the route. With even a relatively short journey taking several days, the humble passengers had the choice of overnight accommodation either in the back of the wagon under the canvas cover or in the stable lofts of the inns at which they stopped. Meals of boiled meat and bread could be taken in the back kitchens of these inns for a modest sum. One traveller disdainfully described the stage wagon as a tedious way to journey only fit for 'women and people of inferior condition', and a Frenchman, Monsieur Soulbrière, who visited England during the reign of Charles II, wrote of how he 'went from Dover to London in a waggon. It was drawn by six horses placed one after another, and driven by a waggoner who walked by the side of them'. (See V.A. Wilson, *The Coaching Era*, 1922.) One of the great pioneers of the stage wagon was Thomas Hobson, who ran such a vehicle between London and Cambridge where he had a contract with the university to carry its mail to the capital.

Despite its shortcomings, the stage wagon helped to make passenger transport more socially acceptable, and the old idea that to travel in a vehicle rather than on horseback was degenerate, effeminate or slothful began to die out. However, it was not until royal patronage, in the form of Queen Elizabeth I of England, was bestowed upon the horse-drawn vehicle that the unsteady progress of the carriage in Europe gained momentum and enjoyed a sudden if belated surge of success.

Chapter 2

The first coach

There are differing opinions as to when the first coach appeared on the streets of London and who introduced it. Certainly, there were coaches in many of the Continental cities like Paris long before they were known here, and one theory is that the first coach was brought from Holland in 1564 as a gift for Queen Elizabeth I by a Dutchman called Guylliam Boonen who later became the royal coachman. It was an ornate-looking vehicle with curtains and plumes but it cannot have been a comfortable conveyance to travel in, for the Queen generally preferred to ride, only using the coach for special occasions. She once confided to the French ambassador that she was 'still suffering aching pains from being knocked about in a coach driven too fast a few days ago'.

There is also evidence, however, that the first coach in England was built in 1555 for the Earl of Rutland by Walter Rippon, a well-known vehicle builder whose firm rose to some prominence in the nineteenth century. In 1564, the same builder produced a 'hollow, turning coach' for Queen Mary, and twenty years later he was responsible for a 'chariot throne with foure pillars behind, to beare a crowne imperiale on the toppe, and before two lower pillars, whereon stood a lion and a dragon, the supporters of the arms of England', in which Queen Elizabeth travelled to St Paul's Cathedral in great pomp to attend a public thanksgiving for the defeat of the Armada. He was also known to have built the first state coach used for the opening of parliament in 1571. The Earl of Arundel is said to have imported a coach from the Low Countries in 1580. When Queen Elizabeth travelled from Ipswich to Norwich in 1589, she apparently rode pillion and held on to the broad belt of the rider to steady herself while her ladies-in-waiting followed behind in coaches. Dr Peter Vannes, the English ambassador to Venice, writing in his report on the death of Lord Courtenay, 18 September 1556, described 'certain wagons called coaches, very shakey and uneasy' – which would suggest that they were suspended in some way, probably from leather braces.

It is believed that the coach may take its name from the small town of Kotsee (pronounced 'cosh') on the road between Budapest and Vienna. Whether this town was significant because it was an important stopping place on the road or because the local craftsmen were responsible for building the first coaches, history does not record, although the latter would seem the most plausible of the varying explanations. It is also possible that the word 'coach' is of Celtic origins, or it could be a derivation of the word 'couch', as there are innumerable references over the ages to closed or canopied vehicles in which people travelled in a reclining position or actually slept. High-ranking Roman officials are known to have used such vehicles for long journeys. By definition, a coach is a vehicle with four wheels, a suspended body, and a roof as part of the integral structure. In practice, the term has been used in a very loose sense since the beginning of the sixteenth century to describe a whole range of vehicles, many of which can have borne little resemblance to a coach. The word 'carriage', on the other hand, was originally used to describe the undercarriage of a vehicle, but it too has been used indiscriminately to refer to horse-drawn vehicles in general until this broad and vague definition has become acceptable.

Such was the popularity of the coach for use not only by the nobility but all those who could afford one, that once again the dreadful state of the roads in England called for government action. Undeterred by the disappointing lack of success of the Highways Act, the government tried to implement a number of statutes and laws with the intention of improving the condition of the roads. Since the heavy stage wagons were the chief culprits in churning up the surfaces, a number of measures were aimed at restricting their use, including a royal proclamation which in 1622 forbade the use of wagons for transporting goods altogether but which was so widely violated that it was soon repealed. Some time later another act tried to ban wagon wheels which were less than nine inches at the rim, the idea being that the broader the wheel the less damage it would do, but this too enjoyed little success. A series of compulsory tolls based on a sliding scale with the broadest wheel paying the lowest levy was flagrantly ignored by the wagoners, and a limitation on the number of horses that could draw a vehicle met a similar fate. Even as late as 1822 an Act was passed prohibiting wheels of less than three inches at the rim, but it stirred up such resentment that it was prudently withdrawn.

Not everyone approved of coaches, however, and in 1601 a bill was proposed, though significantly not passed, seeking to curtail the number of coaches on the roads and forbidding men to ride in them. John Cresset, in *The Grand Concern of England Explained*, 1663, described coaches as 'one of the greatest mischiefs that have happened of late years to the Kingdom', causing those who travel in them to 'become weary and listless when they ride a few miles, unwilling to get on horseback, and unable to endure frost, snow or rain, or to lodge in the fields'. Another writer opposed to coaches deprecated the 'multitude of stage coaches and carriages now travelling on the roads' and a sixteenth-century bishop called coaches 'sin-guilty', while John Taylor, the water poet who turned to writing when his livelihood as a boatman became threatened, accused the coach in *The World Runnes on Wheels* of being a 'close hypocrite, for it hath a cover for any knavery and curtains to veil or shadow any wickedness'. Sir Philip Sidney considered it 'a great disgrace for a young gentleman to be seen riding in the streets in a coach'. So numerous did coaches become that in 1631 the churchwardens and constables of Blackfriars in London complained to the privy council that 'persons of honour and quality that dwell in the parish are restrained by the number of coaches from going out or coming home in seasonable time, to the prejudice of their occasions'.

Despite their critics, coaches continued to increase in popularity until they were a common sight in most of the larger European cities. At first they were restricted to the cities, as country roads were unfit for their use. Although most coaches were privately owned, there were plenty for hire as well, either by the hour or by the day, for which the charge in London, including two horses, was ten shillings. Most of these public hackney coaches had been private town coaches which had become too shabby and worn for their fashionable owners, who sold them to the hackney coach proprietors for a nominal sum. In his book *The English Carriage*, Hugh McCausland gave an account of how many a gentleman's fine town coach 'ended its days on a street rank as a discreditable old ruin with odd wheels of different colours and sizes, moth-eaten hammer cloth, rattling doors still bearing the faded arms of a former owner, and a musty straw-filled interior; the usual accompaniments being a pair of broken-down screws – in harness that had been mended with rope – and an uncouth driver of questionable sobriety'. The name 'hackney' comes from the French word *haquenee*, meaning a horse for hire. Up until the appearance of the hackney coach, the main means of transport in London, as in other European cities built on rivers, had been the boat. Samuel Pepys, petitioning in 1667 for expenses incurred through his work, mentions the substantial cost of coach and ferry hire, which could be as much as six shillings and eightpence a day. The hackney coach curtailed the boat trade severely and stirred up a lot of resentment among the boatmen. According to the fictitious boatman in Henry Peacham's *Coach and Sedan*, a book commenting on London transport and published in 1636, coaches should be thrown into the river, for 'where I was wont to have eight or ten fares in a morning, I now scarce get two the whole day'. Nevertheless, hackney coaches flourished, and in 1634 the first hackney stand, predecessor of the modern taxi rank, was established by a retired mariner, Captain Butler, who had four specially built hackney coaches stationed for hire in the Strand. By the following year, hackney coaches were causing such a disturbance in the streets that Charles I proclaimed that they were only to be used by persons travelling three miles or more out of London. This caused a temporary reduction in their numbers, but it was short-lived and soon the narrow streets were witnessing the first traffic jams. Later, during the reign of Charles II, hackney coaches were prohibited from standing in the streets or driving around slowly in the hope of picking up fares. Instead they had to remain in their yards until summoned. These measures had little effect on their proliferation, as Pepys confirmed in his diary in November 1669, when he wrote, 'Notwithstanding that this was the first day of the King's proclamation against hackney coaches coming into the streets to stand for hire, yet I got one to carry me home,' and a conservative estimate of the time put the number of such vehicles plying for hire in London at nearly 2,500.

During the 1600s the endless demand for coaches was responsible for bringing about many improvements to the basic design, notably in the shape and weight of the body and in the way it was suspended. The early coaches had literally been heavy unsprung boxes on wheels but later vehicles had lighter-weight wooden bodies covered with leather nailed to the frame. Leather curtains or shutters took the place of doors or windows, and cushions and pillows were used for upholstery to compensate for the lack of springs. Later, a low-slung body was suspended by means of leather braces from upright posts which sprang from the axles of both the front and back wheels. Although this was an enormous improvement, the stresses caused by the swaying motion of the body frequently caused the vehicle to drop to bits, particularly on bad roads. Emergency repairs at the roadside were the province of the coachman; he kept a toolbox under his seat, which soon became known as a 'boxseat'. The term 'hammercloth' for the heavy and often ornate cloth which covered the boxseats of some coaches can also be traced to the time when it was essential to carry a hammer and other tools on a vehicle.

The coachbuilder's trade was a busy and most profitable one, described in 1619 as the 'most gainefullest about the towne', and in 1677 the Coachmakers' and Harness Makers' Company received their first charter from Charles II. As many of the first private coach owners were of noble birth or wealthy traders, the vehicles were often lavishly fitted out with sumptuous interiors of buttoned gold cloth that cost almost as much as the coach itself. In 1599, the first glass-windowed coach was seen in Paris and a similar example was built for the Duke of York in 1661, but the constant vibration and jarring easily broke the windows and it was not until several years later that glass windows became common. A number of attempts by coachbuilders to fit steel springs to their vehicles were made, without any lasting success, although Pepys mentions seeing a coach with springs in 1665 which he describes as being 'very fine'. Those coaches built for ceremonial occasions, particularly for the European courts, were sheer masterpieces of baroque design with lavish carving, gilt and decorative emblems, and they were drawn by matched teams of from four to six horses, depending on the formality of the occasion and the need to impress. When the Duke of Northumberland travelled from London to Bath in 1619, he used eight horses and attracted the 'vulgar talk and admiration' of everyone! (See V.A. Wilson, *The Coaching Era*.)

Around 1630 the first stage coaches, as distinct from hackney coaches or the slow and heavy carriers' stage wagons, began to run from London to various destinations in the suburbs, and ten years later the Taxis family started the first regular stage coach service in Germany. In France, public coaches began running during the reign of Charles IX and by 1647 they connected forty-three towns with Paris. Similar services soon operated in most European countries and people began complaining of the traffic which in Paris 'dazzled and deafened the passers-by'. Friedrich Matthias, writing about Vienna in 1680, complained that 'the streets crowded with people, horses and wagons are often a menace to the safety of the pedestrians. The drivers and litter owners keep shouting "Look out, look out" and while you avoid one you bump into another of them.' (Quoted in L. Tarr, *The History of the Carriage.*) Although stage coaches only ran during the dry summer months, the speed at which they rattled along – the horses trotting instead of walking as they had done in the stage wagons – meant that passengers felt every bump and pothole in the roads, and Edward Parker, describing such a journey to London in a letter to his father, dated 1663, wrote, 'This travell has so indisposed mee, that I am resolved never to ride up againe in the cotche.'

The swinging motion of the suspended body was also responsible for making many travellers feel ill, and John Cusset, writing in 1673, asked, 'What additive is this to men's health or business, to ride all day with strangers often times sick, or with diseased persons, or young children crying, to whose humours they are obliged to be subject, forced to bear with, and many times are poisoned with their nasty scents and crippled by the crowd of their boxes and bundles?'

For some years the longest stage-coach run in England was from London to Cambridge but gradually more and more large towns were connected with London by this new means of travelling, and there was even a coach service to Edinburgh, the journey costing four pounds. By 1688, there were stage coaches running from London to eighty-eight different towns and by 1705 this number had increased to one hundred and eighty. In a census of London traffic in 1681, it was recorded that of the one hundred and nineteen coaches mentioned, sixty-five were on long-distance runs and the rest served points within a twenty-five-mile radius of the city.

The reliability and speed of any stage-coach service was largely dependent on the weather, the state of the roads, the skill and enthusiasm of the coachmen, and the possibility of delays caused by accidents, highway-men, or such phenomena as floods or storms. The efficiency of inns on the routes in providing horses for the changeovers and meals for the hungry passengers also had some bearing on whether timetables were adhered to, but the coach proprietors indemnified themselves against all setbacks by advising customers that they travelled 'God willing', and consequently had no grounds for complaint if times of arrival were not met. It is said that in 1689 a Dutchman collapsed and died in the London to Oxford stage coach after having to alight and walk up Shotover Hill, the exertion being too much for his heart. Progress in some coaches was so slow because of the roads that pedlars often kept pace alongside the coach and displayed their wares to the captive passengers. To the simple folk in many of the rural districts, the sight of stage coaches was a revelation when the only vehicles they were familiar with were crudely built farm carts and wagons. People would line the streets and gasp with amazement when the heavily laden coach-and-four rolled by. Unfortunately, the mud on some roads was so bad that the coaches got stuck and the villagers would be both delighted and honoured to help free the vehicle. On particularly bad stretches of road, an extra pair of horses driven by a postillion mounted on the nearside animal sometimes had to be called upon to lend assistance.

Not all contemporary writers disapproved of coaches, however, and in 1673 Edward Chamberlayne wrote of the values of the coach 'where in one may be transported to any place sheltered from foul weather and foul ways, free from endangering of one's health and one's body by hard jogging or over violent motion on horseback; and this not only at the low price of about a shilling for every five miles, but with such velocity and speed in an hour as the foreign post can make but in one day'. (Quoted in D. Mountfield, *The Coaching Age*.) Special fast coaches with speeds of up to five miles an hour were used on some roads, although Charles Matthews, a travelling actor, sarcastically remarked, 'I suppose they are called flying-coaches, because they are the slowest things that ever crawled.' (See V.A. Wilson, *The Coaching Era*.)

The men who drove the hackney and stage coaches soon earned themselves a bad reputation on account of their vulgarity and intimidating behaviour. In the words of one historian, 'every ragamuffin that has a coat to his back thrusts his hands into his pockets, rolls his gait, talks slang and is an embryo coachey'. (Harper, *Stage and Mail in Days of Yore*.) They treated their passengers with little respect, and anyone who failed to tip generously was liable to be bombarded with the most abusive langauge. Their turnout was on the whole very shabby, with the horses badly turned out, the harness dirty, ill-fitting and patched, and the coach itself often little more than a wreck. Very few were skilled coachmen with any consideration for the wretched animals they drove and, as Peacham wrote in 1636, many coach horses could be seen with 'their necks and sides miserably gall'd with collars and traces'. Dressed in grubby coats with thick shawls or scarves around their necks, their feet wrapped in straw to keep them warm, the coachmen's only thought was to get as many fares as possible and they achieved this by flogging their unfortunate animals from one destination to another with little consideration or discretion. The men who drove the stage wagons were no better and were more often chosen for the strength with which they could wield a whip than for their knowledge of horsemanship or geography. Many were heavy drinkers who would think nothing of stopping at every roadside inn for the purpose of imbibing while their poor passengers waited outside in the vehicle. Evidently none of these coachmen had heard of the act which was passed in England in 1604 and which stated that 'the ancient, true and proper use of inns . . . is for receipt, relief and lodging of wayfaring people . . . and not for the entertainment of lewd and idle people to consume their money and time in lewd and drunken manner'. Any passenger having the temerity to complain risked being coarsely insulted or even assaulted. As late as 1837 William Bridges Adams wrote of 'heavy coaches, laden with ill-packed luggage; miserable horses, bound in worse harness; all at the mercy of a red-faced, half-drunken apoplectic coachman, with a wisp of straw for a hatband, and buried under a weight of dirty drab capes and cotton neckcloths'. Some coachmen were in league with highwaymen and got a share of the booty after the coach was robbed, while others conspired with the innkeepers and received a remuneration for guaranteeing a regular clientele who were ill catered for and exorbitantly overcharged.

It soon became the wish of all aspiring citizens to own a coach, although the cost put it out of the reach of most. Samuel Pepys was a regular user of coaches for pleasure as well as business, as may be deduced from an excerpt from his journal describing how he 'took an amorous actress in a hackney coach through the park after the play was done, kissing her a little tentatively'. In 1668, Pepys toured England and was so impressed with the coaches he used that he decided he must own one himself. He purchased a light, 'mighty pretty' four-seater coach second hand, and not wishing to be reliant on hired horses, paid £50 at Smithfield horse market for a pair of black horses. Apart from an unexpected bill for £2 to replace a broken pane of glass in the coach, which suggests that glazed windows were becoming more common, he was well satisfied with his equipage.

The dreadful condition of the roads throughout Europe was still a subject for some concern, but with no system of repair or recognized authority responsible for their upkeep, the prognosis was not good. Heavy wagons carrying up to seventeen hundredweight and pulled by teams of up to ten or twelve horses caused ruts as wide as field ditches over which the stage coaches and trademen's carts bounced and lurched. Defoe, on his tour through Britain in the 1720s, was shocked by 'the great number of horses every year kill'd by the excess of labour in those heavy ways', and even in London as late as 1759 the ruts had to be filled in before George II's coach could progress on its way to the ceremony for the opening of parliament. Accidents caused by horses stumbling or falling on bad pieces of road were very common and in 1769 an Ipswich newspaper reported an inquest on a man who fell from his horse and was 'suffocated by mud and filth'. Accidents always made good material for the newspapers, some of which devoted whole columns to the grim subject.

A partial answer to the problems was the toll road system which was instigated in England in 1633, when the first Turnpike Act was passed. This allowed the setting-up of gates on the Great North Road so that tolls might be collected for the upkeep of roads in Hertfordshire, Cambridgeshire and Huntingdonshire, but it caused such resentment and anger among the road users that it had to be abandoned. The name 'turnpike' came from the long poles or pikes which the first road barriers closely resembled. These barriers were opened or turned to let traffic through, although in later times stout gates were found to be more suitable for the purpose. Towards the end of the seventeenth century, a series of acts were passed which gave the justice of the peace in various districts the power to erect gates across the roads and levy a toll which would be used to pay for road repairs. In all, some two thousand road acts connected with turnpikes and their methods of operating were passed in England. The benefits were not really seen until the Turnpike Trusts, whereby one man or a committee received the right of controlling a stretch of road, were set up. The Trusts employed a toll keeper, who lived in the toll house and was responsible for collecting the tolls and opening and shutting the gate, as well as surveyors and workmen. As toll roads were all separately administered, the charges for road users varied enormously, although most operated a scale which depended on the size and type of vehicle. An average toll for a four-horse wagon with wheel rims of less than six inches would be about a shilling for each time it passed through the toll gate; for similar wagons but with wheel rims of over six inches the charge would be ninepence, and for wagons with even broader wheels which would do less damage to the road the charge would be dropped to about sixpence. With this in mind, one enterprising wagon builder produced a vehicle with broad rollers instead of wheels, but the extra power needed to pull it cancelled out whatever beneficial effects it might have had on the roads. In 1796 Mr Robert Bealson's patent road protector, which was built on the same lines, was unsuccessfully tried and discarded for the same reasons. The mounted post boys who carried the mail were exempt from paying, and they sounded a horn as they approached the gate as a signal for the keeper to clear the way for them. This had to be done quickly so that the mail was not delayed.

Robert Phillips wrote irately in 1737 that 'if the turnpikes were taken down and the roads not touched for seven years, they would be a great deal better than they are now'. Arthur Young, the traveller, was of the opinion that the Bury St Edmunds-to-Sudbury road was 'as infamous a turnpike as ever was beheld' with 'ponds of liquid dirt and a scattering of loose flints just sufficient to lame every horse that moves near them'. (Quoted in D. Mountfield, *The Coaching Age.*) Describing a stretch of road in Lancashire, he wrote of 'ruts which I actually measured four feet deep and floating with mud only from a wet summer', and the roads of Wales he criticized for being 'mere rocky lanes full of hugeous stones as big as one's horse'. Whatever faults the turnpike system had, the fact that in 1750 there were about two hundred Turnpike Trusts in existence and by 1770 this number had risen to five hundred seems to emphasize their overall success. By 1830, ten per cent of all British public roads were turnpikes, a distance of some twenty thousand miles.

During the eighteenth century, the improvements in the art of building not only coaches, but private carriages and tradesmen's vehicles as well, were quite dramatic. The coaches themselves varied in shape according to their country of origin but were all generally heavy and cumbersome, partly on account of the stout beam or 'perch' linking the front and rear axles. The coachman's seat was separate from the body and afforded little comfort, for it was feared that on a soft seat he might fall asleep, to the peril of his passengers. The convex roof of the coach was sometimes fitted with an iron rail around the edge so that trunks or baggage could be secured on top, and a common feature of many was the wicker basket on the back, originally used for holding luggage, but later occupied by poorer passengers who travelled thus for a reduced fare. A German pastor, Karl Philipp Moritz, who travelled through England in 1782, wrote later of the ordeal of coach travel which he experienced from the basket on the back of the vehicle.

> I was just on the point of falling asleep, having had no rest the night before, when on a sudden the coach proceeded at a rapid rate downhill. Then all the boxes, iron-nailed and copper fastened, began, as it were, to dance around me; everything in the basket appeared to be alive, and every moment I received such violent blows that I thought my last hour had come . . . I was obliged to suffer horrible torture for nearly an hour, which seemed to me an eternity. I now write this as a warning to all strangers who are inclined to ride in English stage coaches, or worse still, horror of horrors, a seat in the basket.

The social significance of where the passengers sat on the coach was neatly summed up by the coachmen's instructions for what to do when a steep hill or unusually bad piece of road was encountered. 'First-class passengers keep your seats, second-class passengers get down and walk, third-class passengers get down and push!'

Around 1700 the whip spring came into use, though mainly on private vehicles like the chaises and phaetons which had become very popular, and by 1790 the cee-spring had been invented. Although these early springs represented a major step forward in the development of the carriage, it is probable that they were generally too weak to withstand the violent jolting the vehicles got on all but the very best roads, and it was not until the telegraph and elliptic springs were invented at a later date that the real benefits of the steel spring were appreciated. This did not prevent ambitious coachbuilders trying them out, however, and in 1754 an advertisement announced the running of 'a handsome machine with steel springs for the ease of passengers'. An Edinburgh proprietor advertised a coach with steel springs in the same year, although a Frenchman writing in 1769 was still very sceptical of the advantages of this refinement. The elliptic spring invented by Obadiah Elliott in 1804 brought a revolutionary change in carriage construction by enabling coach builders to produce vehicles without a perch, and this meant lighter, more stylish carriages with greater manoeuvrability. Although most springs were steel or a combination of steel and leather, as in the case of whip and cee-springs, other materials were also experimented with, including whalebone and wood. Not everyone subscribed to the Englishman's preference for sprung vehicles, and in a

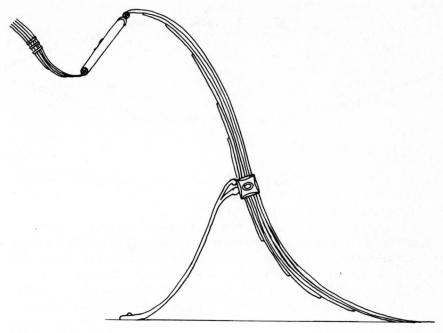

Figure 2 Whip spring.

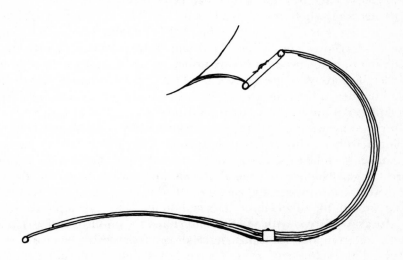

Figure 3 Cee-spring.

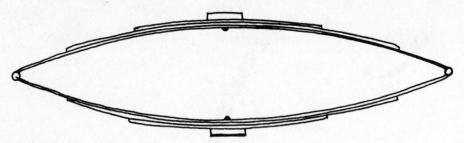

Figure 4 Fully elliptic spring.

foreign newspaper of 1773 a coach builder criticized springs and wrote of the 'healthy violent shaking of a carriage'.

During the late eighteenth and early nineteenth centuries, great progress began to be made in the field of road construction and maintenance, due mainly to the work of three Englishmen who set precedents for the rest of the world to follow. John Metcalfe of Knaresborough in Yorkshire ran his own business as a carrier, even driving a wagon himself on many occasions, despite the fact that he was completely blind. When a new toll road was to be built between Harrogate and Boroughbridge in 1765, Metcalfe persuaded the Trustees to let him build three miles of the road on a trial basis. By finishing the road well within the allotted time and to the complete satisfaction of the Trustees, he earned himself other similar contracts until at one time he was employing four hundred men to work on a nine-mile stretch of road. His success was mainly due to his understanding of the two main fundamental necessities of road building: good drainage and a sound foundation. He achieved this by laying a hard foundation flanked by drainage ditches, with the actual road being constructed of broken stones. His successor (in terms of road building) Thomas Telford's primary contribution was his unquestionable skill in building bridges and canals, but like his contemporary John McAdam, he was also very involved in the building of roads using the same principles as Metcalfe had introduced earlier. Telford was a great advocate of easy gradients and he was the first road builder to level the ground by excavation prior to actually starting building. Both he and McAdam built their roads in three quite separate layers commencing with large interlocking stones. The second layer was composed of small stones and to ensure uniformity an immense workforce of women and children were employed to break the stones into the required size with small hammers. A metal ring was worn on a string around the neck of these patient workers and each stone had to be of a diameter that could pass through the ring before it was laid on the road. The top layer was of coarse gravel spread with a slight camber and the finished road was finally rolled and compounded using a horse-drawn roller before being opened to traffic. The resulting surface could take the heaviest loads without any signs of damage and the worst possible weather without becoming muddy or flooded. The cost of a Telford road was about £1,000 a mile, a huge sum even in those days. The benefits for which Metcalfe, Telford and McAdam were responsible were eventually felt by all road users, and they helped open the way for the mail coaches whose short but highly successful heyday, postumously called the 'golden age', represented one of the most important periods in the history of transport and communications in the world.

Chapter 3
The golden age

The British mail-coach system was the pride of the nation and the envy of the world, and it came into being as a result of the dilemma in which the Post Office found itself towards the end of the eighteenth century when the stage coaches, which by then served most of the main towns and cities, were found to be quicker than the Post Office's official mail carriers, the mounted postboys. People began sending their letters by coach, which was illegal as it defrauded the Post Office of its revenue. The postboys, many of whom were quite elderly, were inefficient for a number of reasons. In the first place, they were instructed to maintain a speed of not more than five miles an hour, although, in trying to improve the service, the Post Office later decreed that six miles an hour should be the ordained speed. The improved stage coaches were much quicker. Most of the postboys, or mailmen as they were later called, were unreliable or dishonest and it was difficult to supervise their activities with any degree of success. They were vulnerable to the depredations of highwaymen, who had become more numerous with the increased road traffic, and like many of the early coachmen, some were not averse to being in league with these roadside thieves. It was evident to the Post Office officials that some reorganization in the whole business of carrying the mail was required, but it was a young businessman from Bath who eventually came up with the solution.

John Palmer's plan was for the mail to be carried by special coaches which, like the postboys, would be exempt from tolls and taxes and which would have right of way over all road users. The work would be contracted out to the same men who ran the stage coaches, who would be paid a standard threepence a mile – no more, in fact, than the postboys had cost. The contractors would be allowed to carry a limited number of passengers as well as parcels to supplement their income. The coachmen and horses were to be supplied by the contractor, but the armed guard who rode on the back of the coach and was responsible for the safe delivery of the mail was to be a Post Office employee. Palmer prophesied that his system would deliver letters in half the time and that this would justify his proposed increase in postal charges. His scheme was presented to the Post Office management, who were apprehensive of the sweeping changes Palmer suggested, and they carefully considered all the advantages and disadvantages of the proposed reform before passing an opinion. Their criticisms were collated into three large volumes and it is highly probable that the mail-coach system would never have got off the ground had Palmer not had a most useful ally in William Pitt whose return to power in 1783 was of great significance in the scheme. Pitt was very keen on Palmer's ideas and he used his considerable influence to overrule the cautious objections of the Post Office. Foremost among these was the general belief that the contractors could never be persuaded to adhere to the strict schedules that were such an integral part of the system. Palmer believed they could, and demonstrated his faith in them by announcing that he required no payment at all for his system unless it proved to be viable and successful, after which he should be entitled to a share of the profits. One of Pitt's reasons for wishing to see the scheme succeed was that the revenue from the increased postal charges would make a more acceptable alternative to his unpopular proposal for a tax on coal. Finally, a trial period commencing in August 1784 was approved and the necessary arrangements were made. As Palmer had forecast, the first mail coach was a resounding success, and it paved the way for a whole network of 'mails', as they were soon known throughout the country. Forty-five years later, when the system had reached its heyday, seven hundred mail coaches covered an incredible twelve thousand miles of English roads every night, and together with the three thousand three hundred stage coaches, they employed one hundred and fifty thousand horses and created jobs for a total of thirty thousand men.

The German mail-coach system was so appalling that Adolph von Schaden, writing in 1822, said of it, 'If your chest is not made of metal, your entrails of copper, and your precious organs of platinum, we strongly recommend you not to undertake a journey by what is called a common mail coach.' The Austrian system was little better, and the French mail coaches or diligences were unattractive, uncomfortable and unsafe. The Spanish mail coaches were similar in design to the heavy and unwieldly French diligences but were drawn by teams of ten or twelve mules decorated with bells.

More successful were the American concord coaches, built by Abbot Downing of Concord, New Hampshire, and operated by such famous companies as the Wells Fargo Co. Sturdily built, with the body slung on thorough-brace springs made of oxhide, and drawn by teams of four or six horses or mules, they were capable of standing the severe joltings they got on the rough overland routes like the 1,913-mile journey from Atchison, Kansas to Placeville, California, for which the passenger fare was $325. The completion of the transcontinental railway in 1870 saw the demise of the American stage coach in favour of steam.

Australia had sported stage coaches since 1821, but it was not until the gold-rush that the need for better public transport resulted in four Americans importing concord coaches into Victoria and setting up the firm of Cobb & Co. in 1853. The venture was a tremendous success and the firm opened two coach-building factories to produce their own design of coaches. By 1870 they employed 6,000 horses to cover 28,000 miles a week. Thirty years later virtually all parts of Australia were covered and by 1930 it had all gone forever. Freeman Cobb, one of the Americans who had helped found the Australian firm of Cobb & Co., also started a coaching firm in South Africa. With a partner, he imported six concord coaches from America and ran a service between Port Elizabeth and the diamond mines at New Rush. Bad roads, expensive fodder and horse sickness doomed the venture and the company went into liquidation in 1874. An Englishman, John A. Gibson, set up a rival firm which enjoyed some success, and the Swedish Zeedenburg Brothers also ran a coach service, using zebras and imported South American mules, which survived until after the Boer War. None, however, rivalled the British mail-coach system for efficiency, speed and reliability.

The Post Office decided that it would be advantageous to have all mail coaches built to a uniform pattern so that they would be instantly recognizable, and this sound decision heralded the beginning of mass production in the coach-building trade. It became possible for a stock of spare parts like wheels, poles and springs to be held at various bases throughout the country so that repairs to coaches could be carried out quickly and with the minimum loss of time. Coach builders submitted designs to the Post Office for consideration, and one or two prototypes were tried out with varying degrees of success. These included several so-called 'safety' coaches which their designers guaranteed could not be tipped over, as well as numerous others with special patent features like automatic brakes. Eventually a patent coach designed by Besant in 1787 and weighing sixteen hundredweight was chosen to be the standard model, and Besant's partner, Vidler of Millbank, Westminster, a noted coach builder, got the contract to build the coaches for the Post Office. The design was not without faults; it was too high and top-heavy, and the coachman's seat was still detached from the body, although the wicker basket at the rear of the vehicle had been replaced with a boot fitted with a hinged door in which the mail was kept. The guard had a seat on top of the boot, and passengers could be accommodated only inside the coach. In 1803, the Post Office relaxed its stringent rules to allow passengers to be carried on the roof of the coach on specially constructed seats, although no one was permitted to sit at the back next to the guard – this was not allowed until the late 1830s. One of Besant's great inventions was the mail axle, a system of securing the wheel to the axle by means of three bolts and a revolving plate, which replaced the primitive linch pins used on earlier coaches to keep the wheels in place. This important invention reduced the number of accidents caused by shed wheels and made coach travel much safer.

Vidler established a contract with the Post Office which ran from 1784 to 1836 and during that period the basic design was amended slightly and

ASKEW'S

KESWICK ᴬᴺᴰ BORROWDALE
⚓ COACH. ⚓

Leave Grange.	Leave Keswick Market-place
9 0	10 15
12 45	2 15
5 0	6 15

The drive between Keswick and Borrowdale, along the margin of Lake Derwentwater, is one of the prettiest in the Lake District. The Bowder Stone (supposed to be the largest piece of detached rock in the world), is within 15 minutes' walk of Grange.

FARE - 9d.

W. ASKEW, Proprietor.

Figure 5 Original timetable card for the Borrowdale coach, *circa* 1900.

such improvements as the fitting of telegraph springs and the addition of a front boot under the boxseat for holding parcels were implemented. Boxseats were also built on to the coach body instead of being a separate structure. According to Matthew Boulton, writing in 1798, the Besant patent coach was so uncomfortable that after a journey in one to Exeter he was not surprised to be told by the landlady at the inn there that 'passengers who arrived every night were in general so ill they were obliged to go supperless to bed; and unless they go back to old-fashioned coaches, long and a little lower, the mail coaches will lose all their custom'. Evidently she was wrong, for the mail coaches flourished and other travellers wrote of the 'marvellous celerity' of this new means of transport. (See Richard Jamieson, *Coaching in the North Country*.) Lord Campbell claimed that the great speed at which passengers were conveyed to London often resulted in some of them dying suddenly of 'an affection of the brain'. All the coaches were actually owned by Vidler, who, although he sold a few at a set price of £140 each, usually hired them out on a mileage basis and was responsible for servicing and repairing them as and when necessary. The coaches were painted in a livery of black and maroon with bright-red wheels and running gear. On each of the quarter panels were painted the stars of the four Great Orders of Knighthood – the Garter, the Thistle, the Bath and St Patrick, and the royal arms were emblazoned on the door panels. The royal cypher was painted in gold on the front boot, and the number of the coach on the hind. As the mails ran through the night, some form of lighting was essential, and coach lamps came into regular use. The first lamps were fuelled with whale oil, which provided poor illumination but was considered more reliable than gas, which had to be stored in special tanks on the roof of the coach. Although the gas lamps gave a better light, they were extremely dangerous in the event of an accident. Harness had to be provided by the contractor, but Palmer, acting on behalf of the Post Office, insisted that it must be of an acceptable standard, and even went as far as arranging the purchase of several sets of harness at fourteen guineas a time which had to be paid for by those contractors whose harness he considered unfit for use. The innkeepers who horsed the mails were not infrequently reminded of their obligations in providing good, sound horses and efficient, experienced staff at the end of each stage, and in 1787 Palmer registered an official complaint because of the poor quality of the horses being provided on the Bristol to London road. Contractors who failed to maintain the high standards the Post Office demanded soon lost their contract and had little chance of getting it back.

Accurate timekeeping was of the utmost importance to the system, and to this end the scarlet-liveried mail guards were issued with an official timepiece sealed in a wooden case which had to be turned over to the postmaster at the end of each stage. If the mail was behind time, the deficit had to be made up on the next stage, a practice that was thwarted when a law was passed in the interests of safety and to prevent reckless driving which decreed that horses must not be galloped. A loophole was found, however, as the mail was still within the law providing one horse was trotting even if the other three were galloping. This vague rule gave rise to the inclusion in the team of a very fast trotter, nicknamed a 'parliamentary' horse, so that the coach could maintain fast speeds without breaking the law. Contractors or mail guards responsible for unpunctuality were liable to get a curt circular from the Superintendant of Mailcoaches.

I am commanded by the Postmasters General to inform you that the time lost on your ground between _____ and _____ by the mail coach, as it was on its way to _____ was _____ minutes; and I am further directed to desire you will immediately give such orders that time may be kept, for it is only to such as keep time, and do their duty well, the additional mileage can be given.

Thomas Hasket, who held the post of Superintendent from 1792 to 1817, wrote the following note to the guard reprimanding him for running late on account of passengers lingering over their meal at an inn.

Stick to your time bill, and never mind what the passengers say respecting waiting over time. Is it not the fault of the landlord to keep them so long? Some day, when you have waited a considerable time (suppose five or eight minutes longer than is allowed on the bill) drive away and leave them behind. Only take care you have witness that you called them out two or three times. Then let them get forward how they can.

The guard was also supplied with a cutlass and a brace of pistols and a blunderbuss with which to protect the mail, although there is no record anywhere of his having to use them for this purpose. Instead, they frequently discharged the blunderbuss at farm animals or stray dogs, to the alarm of passengers, until things got so bad that an act of parliament was passed in 1811 forbidding the firing of the blunderbuss except in defence, offenders being liable to a fine of five pounds. Another item of standard equipment was the three-foot-long coach horn, sometimes called the 'yard of tin', on which the guard sounded such calls as 'clear the road', 'slacken pace', and 'change horses'. Some guards carried a key bugle, which was a more versatile instrument, even though the Post Office had banned its use as they felt it was too frivolous. Many guards still secretly carried one and entertained the passengers on long journeys by playing popular tunes like 'Oh dear, what can the matter be'.

Every guard also received a list of twenty-six instructions pertaining to his duties, distributed in November 1829. It included such directions as: 'The guard is entrusted with the care of the letter bags, and he is to be answerable at his peril for the security, safe conduct and delivery of them sealed,' and warnings to remind him that 'drunkenness, or disobedience of official orders, will be punished with dismissal'. The list went on to state that 'if the mail coach should fall between stage and stage, the guard is to press one of the mail coach horses, and ride on to the next stage with it', and 'if in travelling from London an accident happens, he is to use all proper expedition in repairing the coach, and if it cannot be done in an hour or an hour and a half, as the circumstances of that particular road will allow, the guard must take chaise to forward the mail'.

Most of the coach proprietors were innkeepers, thus having two strings to their bow, and some of the most successful contractors had more than one inn, as was the case with William Chaplin, the son of a Rochester coachman, who built up a vast business concern that around 1838 was known to operate nearly two hundred coaches around the country. He started out as a horse dealer, then graduated to running coaches from his well-known inn, The Swan with Two Necks, in London, and eventually owned something like eighteen hundred horses and employed two thousand people as well as owning five London inns. Often coach services were the joint venture of two or more partners who owned some of the inns or stopping places on the route and came to a business agreement with the others. The most expensive and difficult part of the whole business was the horsing of coaches, and even the biggest coaching contractors were at the

mercy of the innkeepers on their routes who were paid a fixed amount
annually to provide suitable horses. In areas where inns were plentiful the
contractors could negotiate for the best terms, but where a solitary inn had
the monopoly of a stretch of road the innkeeper could overcharge with
impunity, knowing that his services were essential if the coaches were to be
kept running. The efficiency of the innkeepers in providing horses varied
enormously despite the constant vigilance of the Post Office. One
coachman who drove the Tantivy between Oxford and Birmingham
complained that the horses provided at Stratford-upon-Avon were so old
that they were probably owned by Shakespeare, while on many of the night
runs blind, lame or diseased horses were often provided under cover of
darkness by unscrupulous innkeepers.

The average cost of a coach horse was about twenty-five pounds and they
were generally provided by dealers who specialized in this lucrative section
of the market. The length of a coach horse's working life depended largely
on the length and strenuousness of the stages it worked. The usual distance
was ten miles, and most worked a stage a day with the fourth day off as a
rest, but few lasted longer than six or seven years on account of the excessive
hard work, and many were finished after four years. The lucky ones saw out
their days pulling tradesmen's vehicles, which generally meant lighter
work; the rest went to the slaughter houses. Although for town work the
teams were always matched for colour, on country runs it was quite
common to have unmatched or 'mixed' teams and some contractors liked to
have a coloured or grey horse in the lead as they showed up well on night
runs. Most horses had their tails docked so that there was no chance of a
horse getting its tail over a rein and causing an accident. The cost of keeping
a coach horse was about nineteen shillings a week, this figure including
feeding, shoeing and any veterinary expenses. The term 'to die in harness'
comes from these times, for many horses did simply die from overwork and
exhaustion. In 1821, on one mail-coach route alone, twenty horses dropped
dead as a result of their exertions.

In contrast to his shabbily dressed and surly predecessor, the coachman
of the 'golden age' was noted not only for his skill on the boxseat but also for
his immaculate appearance and polite manner. Fashionably dressed in a
well-cut boxcloth coat and white beaver hat, he was an autocrat whose
word was law with regard to the harnessing of the horses and the loading of
the coach, and all those with whom he was associated treated him with
great respect. He was paid something in the region of a sovereign a week,
double what was paid to the guard, although both supplemented their
incomes quite substantially with tips and by undertaking small commis-
sions like the safe delivery of love letters or small packages. Some coachmen
also earned a little extra by teaching young gentlemen how to drive a team,
even though this was strictly banned by the Post Office because it put both
the mail and the passengers in potential danger as a result of the trainee's
incompetence. Any coachman caught allowing someone else to drive was

immediately dismissed and also fined up to ten pounds at the discretion of the magistrates. For the privilege of the professional coachman's advice and tuition, the wealthy young men 'when bidding them farewell would give them a guinea or half a guinea, and shake them by the hand'. Many coachmen began their careers as postboys and later aspired to the boxseat, but others came from altogether different backgrounds. One was Sir Vincent Cotton, a young baronet, who took to driving professionally after he had squandered his inheritance of five thousand pounds per annum on gambling and women, and another gentleman coachman was Sackville Gwynne, who 'ran through all his property, and died in Liverpool where he was driving a cab'. (See D. Mountfield, *The Coaching Age*.)

Coachmen had, of necessity, to be men of strong constitution, as their work was hard and tiring, and they were obliged to endure everything from scorching sunshine to thunderstorms and snowdrifts while on the boxseat. Many suffered from arthritis of the hands, an affliction they ironically referred to as 'coachman's cramp'. Some met their deaths on the boxseat in diverse ways like William Upfold, or 'Unlucky Upfold' as his friends called him, who had been a coachman for thirty-five years before a series of unfortunate accidents began to tarnish his reputation and he was eventually killed when his coach overturned at Salvington.

For a time, an annual coach parade was held at Millbank each May Day, and all the large London coach proprietors turned out to show off their coaches, horses, harness and staff. According to J.K. Fowler, the author of *Echoes of Old Country Life*, 'The coaches and harness were either new or newly painted and furnished, the horses in the pink of condition and beauty, the coachmen and guards in new liveries of scarlet and gold, each proprietor vieing with his opponent in an endeavour to produce the most perfect turnout.' The parade took the form of a procession from Westminster, through the Strand, Fleet Street, past the Old Bailey, to the General Post Office where it finished, and people lined the streets to watch. With the demise of coaching, the parade was discontinued and never to be revived.

Chapter 4
Behind the scenes

The outstanding success of the mail-coach system was largely responsible for bringing into prominence the coach builders, wheelwrights, horse dealers, jobmasters, harness makers and other traders who were to assume positions of unparalleled importance during the nineteenth century. As more people travelled both for business and pleasure, the demand for new and specialized types of vehicles, as well as horses to pull them, was suddenly insatiable, and in the wake of the horse-and-carriage suppliers and builders came a whole army of grooms, ostlers, stable-boys and farriers to service this great horse-powered industry.

From the end of the eighteenth century the coach builder's art began to blossom as new technology and materials were applied to new designs, and it was during this period that the English carriage became a byword for quality and craftsmanship, with English carriage builders setting the precedent for the rest of the world. In *A Treatise on Carriages*, published in 1794, William Felton stated that 'coachbuilding had been in a gradual state of improvement for half a century past, and has now arrived to a very high degree of perfection, with respect to the beauty, strength and elegance of our carriages', while a few years later a British government official wrote that in 'the variety of construction of public carriages for the conveyance of passengers London excels all other places'. The Society of Arts had embarked upon a policy of awarding prizes for developments in carriage building and in 1769 they gave twenty guineas to Mr J. Jacobs for his improvements to coach springs and sixty guineas to Mr T. Hunt for improving the methods of putting tyres on wheels. Around 1800 the first gigs appeared on the roads, and these were followed by an endless range of phaetons, dogcarts and other vehicles intended to serve every conceivable purpose. The old clumsy and poorly designed vehicles were quickly being replaced by light, elegant and comfortable vehicles, and this radical change was attributable not only to the superiority of English roads in comparison to those of other European countries but also to the imagination of the English carriage designers and their talent for introducing daring innovations. In 1770, Monsieur Rubo, a Frenchman, wrote that provided vehicles were English that was sufficient 'to make all the world desire to have them'. The Emperor of China was an exception, for when the British envoy to China presented him with a state coach on behalf of His British Majesty, the Chinese sovereign refused the gift, for he considered it wrong for the coachman to sit in front of and higher than the Emperor, and anyway he 'set no value on objects strange and ingenious'!

In *A Treatise on Carriages*, 1794, Felton, the famous eighteenth-century spokesman for the carriage trade, expressed the opinion that:

> The carriage should always be built to suit the place it is destined for; the builder must therefore consider whether the vehicle is meant for town, country or the continent; whether it would be heavily loaded, or used on stony or smooth roads; he must also bear in mind that jolting on cobblestones in town practically shakes the framework of a carriage asunder.

Accordingly, coach builders turned out vehicles as diverse as dress chariots, built for formal use, and travelling wagons built 'on two and four wheels for exploring and travelling purposes in Africa and South America . . . the interior can be fitted up with lockers, mattresses, sleeping hammocks, etc., as required, and they are made for horse and bullock draught'. In his book *Modern Carriages*, Sir Walter Gilbey reminds us that 'fashion is as fickle and uncertain in the shape of a carriage as it is in other matters'. It became common practice to order vehicles to meet individual preferences, and a president of the Institute of British Carriage Manufacturers expressed his disdain for 'the new class of owner who no longer has a carriage built to his precise specifications'. (J. Phillipson, *The Art and Craft of Coach-building*, 1897.) Carriages became the distinguishing mark of the taste and social status of the owner. Statistics reveal that in 1814 there were sixty thousand private vehicles in regular use in England, but by 1900 the figure had increased to five hundred thousand.

Surprisingly, most of the changes in the appearance of carriages effected during the nineteenth century were superficial, and few structural innovations were introduced. The old type of axle fitted with a linch pin to keep the wheel in place became obsolete after about 1840 and was replaced either by the mail axle, named after the mail coaches on which it was first used, or the collinge axle, named after its inventor. The collinge axle was first introduced in 1792 and its value lay not only in its reliability but also in the fact that it required greasing less frequently and was thus a great timesaver. It was estimated that mail axles needed greasing every eighty to a hundred miles. The cylindrical arm of the collinge axle had an oil groove running longitudinally to ensure a constant supply of lubricant. The axle was actually held on by a collet, two nuts and a split pin, and a hubcap covered the nuts and acted as a reservoir for grease as well as helping to keep out dirt and moisture. A better system of attaching a wheel to an axle was never discovered. The outdated form of front axle, which pivoted on a centre pin bolting the axle to the vehicle body or fore-end of the wooden perch, was never very practical as this arrangement was liable to break

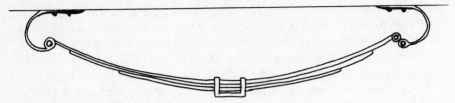

Figure 6 Side, semi-elliptic, horizontal or grasshopper spring.

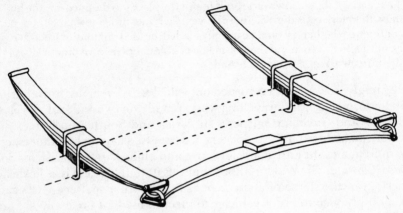

Figure 7 Dennett spring.

under the pressure applied when turning, and the centre bolts also wore out very quickly. It was replaced by a simple device called a 'turntable' or 'fifth wheel', which comprised two circular plates, one attached to the front axle and the other to the underside of the front of the vehicle; these bolted together in the centre and rotated against each other. Not only did this system greatly reduce the likelihood of breakages as the pressure was more evenly distributed, it also facilitated turning and solved the problems of friction and wear and the necessity for the regular replacement of parts.

New forms of springing also came into use and the immensely popular elliptic spring was joined by side or semi-elliptic springs and dennett springs, an arrangement of three springs supposedly named after the singing trio of sisters of that name. Some enterprising firms like Morgan's of London devised their own types of springs – the Morgan spring being a cross between the elliptic and cee-spring. An important innovation was that of rubber tyres which, in the words of one coach builder, were 'invaluable and indispensable for invalids'. (Trade catalogue for Wilsons of Lindale, Cumbria.) Up until then, all tyres had been metal hoops which were fitted to the wheel when red hot and shrunk on by immersing in cold water. Although metal tyres were very hardwearing, they were noisy when the vehicle was in motion. Rubber tyres, which were quiet as well as affording a slight cushioning effect, were made from caoutchouc which was first imported from South America towards the end of the eighteenth century and used for waterproofing cloth. Brakes took some time to gain acceptance, being first employed in the form of skid-pans placed under the wheels of coaches. Hand brakes with a mechanism that applied a brake shoe, usually made of chestnut wood, to the rear wheels of a vehicle, came in later and were generally only fitted to four-wheeled carriages, although a few two-wheeled vehicles also had them. Foot brakes never achieved great popularity. The Victorians were great inventors and produced an incalculable number of patent devices for carriages, the majority of which unfortunately came too late to be of any lasting value, for by the time Queen Victoria died the carriage had rivals in steam and internal combustion engines. Perhaps the most original invention of the nineteenth century was the equirotal phaeton, designed and built by William Bridges Adams, the coach builder, engineer and author. Its chief characteristic was that the body was hinged at the centre so that when the horse or horses turned the driver was always directly behind them, while the rear part of the vehicle articulated on a central pivot. Adams claimed that such a vehicle could be turned in the narrowest streets. The kingpin connecting the two halves of the vehicle could also be removed and the front half driven like a two-wheeled vehicle. Undeterred by the general lack of interest shown in his invention, Adams went on to design and build equirotal omnibuses, coaches and town chariots, the latter even installed with a simple central-heating system involving water pipes and an oil heater.

One of the reasons for the success of the English coach builders was their insistence upon using only top quality materials, and to this end they imported a great deal of timber as well as using traditional home-grown woods. The expansion of Britain's foreign trade, especially with America and the West Indies, played an important part in keeping the cost of imported materials down to a viable level, as well as providing new openings for English coach builders to export their product. Russian tsars, American ministers, Indian maharajahs as well as heads of state and members of old-established European royal families bought their carriages in London, knowing them to be the best. All timber had to be well seasoned before it could be used, and some firms achieved this by leaving wood destined to become wheel hubs, felloes and spokes in running water for up to two months. For the framework of carriages, English ash was favoured, as it is strong, light yet easily bent, but for the panels Spanish or Honduras mahogany was preferred, as it could be obtained in widths of up to four feet and was straight-grained in texture and free from knots and blemishes. For floors and footboards, deal or American ash was often used, while another imported wood, American pine, was chosen for the roofs of carriages. Lancewood, a springy but brittle wood imported from the West Indies in the form of narrow poles of up to twenty feet in length, was usually selected for the making of shafts. Although lancewood could be slightly bent for the production of shaped shafts, this tended to weaken it, and when curved shafts came into vogue in later times it was replaced with other woods, including ash and hickory. A few early gigs were built with lancewood springs carved to give them the appearance, when painted, of steel leaf springs.

The number of different tradesmen and craftsmen necessary to build a carriage was quite astounding and their work demanded a wide range of skills as well as sound judgement and great patience. Most learned their skills through long apprenticeships on the shop floor. Coach building firms varied in size from those with large city factories to humble village concerns, and there was even a lady coach builder, Anne Cowburn, whose firm occupied premises in Manchester. As most carriages were individually built, it was difficult to operate mass-production methods in the trade, although Vidler, the mail-coach builder, had succeeded to a limited extent, as his vehicles were manufactured identically. Writing in 1837, William Bridges Adams could easily have been commenting on Vidler's system in *English Pleasure Carriages*, 1837, when he wrote, 'It may be said that stage coaches are numerous enough to employ a well-ordered factory, with steam and machinery; but whoever takes the trouble to examine them will find that, with the exception of the preparation of their crude iron and similar material, they are entirely the result of uncertain handicraft labour of various degrees of skill.' The notion of mass production was generally frowned upon as being a substitute for good workmanship and John Philipson, author of *The Technicalities of the Art of Coach Body Building*, expressed the opinion that because of mass production, 'coachbuilding in some places appears to consist of little more than assembling the various parts together'.

Of the tradesmen employed in the coach builder's factory, the body makers were the most skilled and highly paid, sometimes earning up to nine or ten pounds a week on piece rate. For this, they worked long sixteen-hour days, working from drawings to produce masterpieces of joinery, and often taking their meals at the workbench. Owing to the nature of their work, there were frequently periods in between jobs when they were unemployed and therefore unpaid, so taking the year as a whole their average weekly wage was more in the region of four pounds. This was still one or two pounds more than the weekly earnings of the body makers, who built the chassis and were second only to the carriage makers in terms of skill. Their work was less demanding, although neatness and accuracy were still essential. The ironwork for the carriage bodies was the responsibility of the coachsmiths, who worked in very hot conditions hammering out the parts then filing them smooth, to make door hinges, lamp brackets and handles. The smiths had to be strong, and their labours earned them between thirty shillings and two pounds per week. The trimmers made all the upholstery, using such materials as silk, morocco leather, whipcord and canvas, but they were also responsible for covering dashboards, splashboards and hoods with heavy-duty leather and sewing the leather on to the ends of shafts and poles. Coach painters were very important, as the whole appearance of a carriage could depend on their work. In addition to having an eye for colour and knowing which colours went well together, they had to know the durability of different paints and how a layer of varnish might affect them. Another of their jobs was matching colours when a vehicle needed to be fitted with a new panel or door and the new paint had to be matched with the rest of the carriage. The process of painting a vehicle required immense patience and a great deal of time, for as many as twenty coats of primer, paint and varnish would be applied in order to get the correct depth of colour and a perfectly smooth surface. The aim of the numerous coats of primer was to fill the grain of the wood, and each coat would be carefully rubbed down with pumice stone and water. The actual body paint would then be applied in consecutive coats, each allowed to dry completely then lightly sandpapered before the top coat was applied. This was protected by a number of coats of fine copal varnish, all but the last rubbed down with mild abrasive paste applied with a cloth. Many family carriages had the coat of arms painted on to the door panels and this was done by a heraldic painter who would generally work freelance. As a rule, vehicles for town use were painted, whereas vehicles for country use were stained and varnished.

As well as the tradesmen, a number of wood sawyers and labourers were employed in most coach builders' shops to assist the tradesmen as required. Their work was lowly and repetitive and their wages were correspondingly low. Although some firms employed men of other trades, it became increasingly widespread practice for much of the work to be subcontracted. Specialist firms appeared, like William E. Cary of Manchester, whose Redbank works established in 1848 produced nothing but carriage axles and springs of every imaginable design, and Gadsons, the wholesale coach ironmongers of London, who advertised that they could 'supply everything required by the coach, cart and van builder'. Birmingham was for a long time the centre of the ironmongers' trade, with firms like Joseph Gibson of West Bromwich distributing their axles all over Great Britain. The American firm of G.F. Kimball of New Haven, Connecticut, not only manufactured carriage wheels but sold the machinery for others to do likewise. There were a great many wheelwrights producing everything from light gig wheels to very heavy wagon wheels, and many were under contract to supply all the requirements of particular coach builders. Towards the end of the nineteenth century, large numbers of wheels were imported into Europe from America where mass production in the form of automatic lathes could turn out two hundred and seventy spokes an hour. Other subcontractors included lace makers, blind makers, and the craftsmen who produced many of the beautiful ivory fittings for carriage interiors, and there were also a multitude of workers indirectly involved, preparing paints and varnishes, weaving fabrics, making glue and tanning leather.

Of the two thousand or so coach-building firms known to be in operation in England in the second half of the nineteenth century, the most fashionable ones tended to be concentrated in London, although most sizeable towns sported at least one or two. Oxford at this time had twenty-four. Some firms, like Holland and Holland of London, were famous for their road coaches, while others like Lawton of Liverpool were noted for their Liverpool gigs. Although London-built vehicles were generally believed to be the best, many very fine vehicles were turned out by country coach builders, some of whom sent their carriages to the capital to be sold as London-built. Brewsters of New York and Million & Guiet of Paris were both top coach builders in their respective countries, although the carriages they produced were generally based on London designs. Many leading coach builders exhibited their new designs abroad at special coach and carriage exhibitions held in such places as Paris, Lisbon and New York, with the hope of attracting foreign buyers.

As well as producing new carriages to order, many coach-building firms stocked a selection of quality second-hand vehicles too, most of which would have been taken in part exchange for new vehicles. Offords, the famous London coach builders who for twelve years supplied carriages to the United States ministers, were one such firm, and they proudly advertised 'a large, well seasoned stock of both new and second hand carriages of all kinds for sale, hire and exchange. Good second hand carriages wanted.' There were also innumerable sales where carriages could be purchased, and one of the most famous was Tattersalls in London where 'every type of pleasure vehicle seems to be on view, duly numbered in lots for the hammer'. There were also two notorious carriage bazaars at Belgravia and Baker Street where carriage brokers, the forerunners of the second-hand car salesmen of modern times, offered dozens of vehicles, some genuine, most not, at bargain prices. These astute dealers were masters at producing smart-looking carriages for such sales, but all too often they had been painted specially for the bazaar and beneath their shining exteriors hid unsound wood or damaged and inadequately repaired panels.

It was usual for carriage owners to replace their vehicles periodically, for in spite of the fine workmanship that went into the building and the meticulous care the carriage received, regular use soon made them shabby, and at a time when appearances meant so much, this could not be tolerated. Vehicles were serviced annually and repainted every three or four years, depending on how often they were used and for what purpose. This was undertaken by the coach builder, who would also replace tyres and leatherwork, revarnish the vehicle or renew the lining as required, and charge exorbitantly for it, even adding a storage fee if the owner did not collect his carriage immediately. With refurbishing costing as much as two-thirds of the price of a new vehicle, it made good sense to replace vehicles every four to five years, and coach builders always found the most plausible excuses for making very poor offers for trade-in vehicles. The firm of Hopkinsons of High Holborn, London, quoted the Earl of Radnor nearly six hundred pounds as the cost of a new full-dress coach in 1842, but could only offer him a paltry fifteen pounds for his travelling chariot in part-exchange. As an inducement to customers, hire purchase was introduced into the retail trade and coach builders' advertisements often stated both the cash and hire-purchase prices. A cheaper method of acquiring a suitable vehicle was to hire one, and most coach builders of any size and reputation advertised this service. By the mid-nineteenth century, a brougham painted in the customer's own choice of livery and even with his crest on the panels could be hired for as little as between thirty and forty pounds per year, although longer and shorter hiring contracts could also be arranged. It was possible to hire carriages only for special occasions like weddings, smart social functions and race meetings, and with this in mind, many coach builders formed special business partnerships with jobmasters who could provide the horses to draw the vehicle.

The first true jobmasters were the innkeepers who supplied horses for the post chaises and stage coaches that plied the roads towards the end of the eighteenth century. As a profession, they became increasingly numerous in the eighteen hundreds, until by late Victorian times there were nearly one hundred and fifty jobmasters in London alone, and they 'horsed' almost everything from the Queen's carriages to the doctor's brougham and the coalman's cart. They could provide horses and vehicles for every possible purpose, including weddings and funerals, and some of the larger firms supplied horses on contract for both businesses and private individuals. For the Jubilee celebrations of 1887, Queen Victoria was obliged to avail herself of the services of one of the leading London jobmasters, who duly provided twenty-five landaus each drawn by a pair of greys for the use of foreign royalty. At the other end of the scale, jobmasters also provided charabancs for the annual staff outings from the factories and mills that the growth of British industry had caused to prosper.

The advantage in hiring from a jobmaster as opposed to owning the horses or vehicles oneself were manifold. The heavy initial cost of purchasing the horses, carriages and harness was borne by the jobmaster, who, by bulk buying and judicious administration, could keep his charges on a level with the expenses of a private owner. He could provide a coachman if called upon, or liveried footmen for a formal occasion, or if the horses were being stabled at the customer's premises, grooms and a stable-boy. Around 1890, it cost about two hundred pounds a year to maintain a brougham in London, but a jobmaster could provide the brougham, horse, harness, a coachman, and feed and shoe the horse for two hundred and ten pounds a year without the customer having even to consider initial outlay or depreciation. If any part of the equipage proved unsuitable it could be replaced, and Thomas Tilling, the largest of the London jobmasters, guaranteed that 'he could replace a lame horse, a broken carriage or a drunken coachman within the hour'.

Dick Hunt began his career as a jobmaster by purchasing an established business in Hove; he took over 'about twelve horses, some very good liveries and six licensed landaus'. In his memoirs he recalled, 'I would supply a French shaped Victoria with rubber tyres, a coachman in breeches and boots, a horse worth fifty pounds in the trade, brass mounted harness and rosebuds in the bridle for ten shillings and sixpence for two hours . . . doctors were among my principal customers.' Thomas Tilling had a more humble start in the business. He arrived in London in 1847 at the age of twenty-two with nothing but a grey mare called Kitty and thirty pounds with which to set himself up in business. Sixty years later his firm employed seven thousand horses in a nationwide business empire. He supplied commercial firms with heavy cart-horses, businessmen with broughams, fashionable ladies with park phaetons, and ran his own fleet of hansom cabs and omnibuses in addition to providing the horse power for both the police and the fire brigade. According to W. J. Gordon, the author of *The Horse World of London*, published in 1893, the firm of Thomas Tilling averaged 'half a dozen weddings a day all the year round, Sundays excepted for Sunday is not a favourite marriage day among the folks who patronise the jobmaster'. Tilling's huge premises at Peckham never closed, and he had so many horses in and around London that he was responsible for feeding that he had carts delivering forage to private stables once a week. One of the advantages of horsing so many varied concerns was that if a horse was found to be unsuitable for one job it could be transferred to another, for the jobmaster's motto was 'hard work cures all ills'.

The jobmaster employed a considerable number of men as grooms, coachmen and farriers, although many of the latter were actually self-employed and under contract to the jobmaster. By 1872, there were over three hundred and fifty farriers in London alone. It is recorded that in a six-month period, one firm of farriers with three shoeing shops 'put on 306,401 shoes, made 20,456 and removed 4,470'. Of the jobmaster's workforce, the majority were regular employees who were paid a weekly wage of around thirty shillings, although those who drove the cabs and omnibuses could expect to add to this considerably with gratuities. The dishonest ones further supplemented their incomes by 'shouldering' or misappropriating a percentage of the fares.

The prodigious task of finding horses to meet the great demand and in sufficient numbers fell to the horse dealers, or copers, as they were known, who made a good living buying and selling to every section of the horse world. Although some of the larger jobmasters employed their own buyers to keep them supplied with suitable young horses, most relied upon the services of a dealer. In a profession where reputations could be made or lost on a misdeal, the majority of dealers were reputable men, but a few, like their contemporaries in the carriage trade, were not averse to a shady deal and their methods of deceiving those with little knowledge were many. A quiet or lazy horse would be livened up by standing it in cold water or in a dark stable until the customer arrived, at which time the poor animal would be led out, startled and prancing, into the bright light. Fiery or difficult

Egyptian chariot, *circa* 1400 BC. Assembled ɔm as many as fifty component parts held gether with wooden nails, pins and glue, these ɔng but extremely light vehicles ranged from ilitarian examples to the richly gilded chariots inlaid with semi-precious stones and stained glass, drawn by ornately harnessed, ostrich-plumed horses and used by the Pharoahs for ceremonial purposes.

Two-wheeled cart with studded wheels, loaded ith corn: an illustration from the Lutrell psalter, *ca* 1338. There was a general disdain during the ʋelfth and thirteenth centuries for riding in carts owing to the state of the roads and the fact that carts were used to carry those condemned to death to the scaffold; people did not like the associations.

3 The original brougham designed by Lord Brougham and built by Messrs Robinson and Cook in 1838. In 1840 Lord Brougham sold his much-copied prototype to Sir William Foulis and subsequent owners included Lord Henry Bentinck and Earl Bathurst. Gladstone and Disraeli were amongst those who used it. The vehicle is now on exhibition at the Science Museum, London.

4 *Below* Royal Mail coach, *circa* 1820, designed by John Besant and built by Vidler of Westminster, London. Weighing sixteen hundredweight and built to a uniform pattern at the request of the Post Office to facilitate the supply of spare parts, these famous vehicles heralded the beginning of mass-production in the coach-building trade.

American concord coach built by The Abbot
owning Co. of Concord, New Hampshire, *circa*
75. These robust vehicles, which were drawn
teams of four or six horses or mules, were
ng on oxhide thorough-brace springs to
thstand the severe joltings they got on the
ugh overland routes like the 1,913-mile journey
om Atchison, Kansas to Placeville, California.

6 *Below* Skeleton brake (sometimes spelt break)
used for the breaking and training of young
horses. The pupil would be harnessed alongside
an older, experienced horse called a
'schoolmaster' and made to go. The high boxseat
was positioned out of the way of kicking hoofs
and the pole and splinter bar were leather-
covered for added protection.

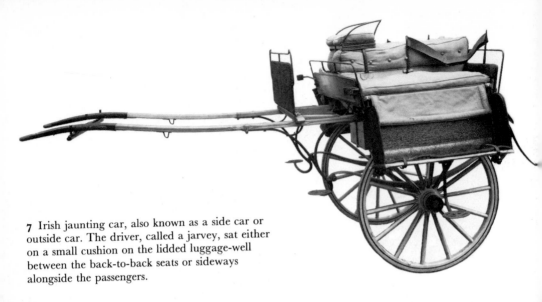

7 Irish jaunting car, also known as a side car or
outside car. The driver, called a jarvey, sat either
on a small cushion on the lidded luggage-well
between the back-to-back seats or sideways
alongside the passengers.

8 American cabriolet sleigh built by the French
Carriage Co., Boston, *circa* 1890. This vehicle is
particularly unusual as it is provided with springs,
allowing each runner to operate independently of
the others thereby ensuring a smooth ride over
the roughest ground.

South African cape cart, one of the few types of
o-wheeled vehicle designed to be drawn by a
ir of horses or oxen, the pole being supported
 special cape cart harness with a yoke. The
me is derived from the Cape of Good Hope
ere the vehicle was first introduced by Dutch
tlers.

Wheelwrights at work hooping wheels, *circa*
0. The metal tyres or hoops were slipped over
 wheel while hot, then cooled by dousing with
d water. As the tyre cooled, it shrank and held
 felloes and spokes firmly together.

11 Primitive hearse of a type used in rural areas in the north of England until comparatively recently. Many hearses were very ornately carved with engraved glass side-panels and silver fittings. Hearses in which children were carried were painted white instead of the customary black.

12 *Below* Grantham Dairy Company's prize-winning milk float, *circa* 1900. Milk floats were among the first vehicles to have rubber tyres so that they made the minimum of noise when making early-morning deliveries. The horses learnt to walk from door to door themselves as deliveries were being made.

Hansom cab built by Wilkinson of Liverpool, circa 1890. These distinctive vehicles, known as the gondolas of London, were thought to be rather dashing and no lady would risk her reputation by riding in one, especially alone. Although essentially a public service vehicle, a few were privately owned and used.

14 *Below* American grocer's delivery sleigh, *circa* 1880, which was used to deliver groceries and dairy produce to New Englanders during the winter months when door-to-door deliveries were particularly welcome.

15 Sefton landau built by Holland & Holland of London. Landaus were originally introduced from Germany but an improved canoe-shaped design which could be drawn by one horse was built by Messrs Hooper for the Earl of Sefton and named after him. A squarer, angular version built for the Earl of Shelburne bears his name.

16 *Below* Four-wheeled dogcart built by Thompsons of Perth, Scotland. Dogcarts often had louvred or slatted sides to provide ventilation for the sporting dogs that were carried under the seats on their way to hunts, shooots or coursing matches – hence their name.

17 Sociable, built by Silk & Son of London. Although sociables were first used around 1700, the design was much improved upon in later times and by the end of the nineteenth century they were favoured as ladies' carriages for park driving in the summer. The name results from the vis-à-vis seating.

18 *Below* Carrier's wagon, *circa* 1900. These equipages provided a service of sorts for goods and passengers between towns. To say of a country girl in London that she had 'come up with the carrier' was to imply that she was no better than she ought to be.

19 Oil delivery tanker, *circa* 1900. Although most tankers were substantial four-wheeled vehicles drawn by a pair of horses, much smaller two-wheeled examples were sometimes used for delivering paraffin in rural areas.

20 *Below* Pair horse wagonette, *circa* 1910. Introduced from the Continent by the Prince Consort in 1845, the wagonette was described as being a 'perfect open family carriage'. One was often kept on country estates for general use.

21 Three-horse charabanc, *circa* 1900. The name comes from the French, meaning 'car with benches', and the first charabanc to appear in England was presented to Queen Victoria by King Louis Phillipe of France in 1842. Difficult horses were often worked in the centre or 'pin' position to settle them down.

22 *Below* Horse-drawn tram, *circa* 1905. A laden tram could weigh in excess of five tons and the strain of continually stopping and starting was very hard on the horses, whose working lives rarely spanned more than three or four years.

23 Mrs J. DuBois driving a pair of Morgan horse mares to a salon trap built by Flandrau & Co. of New York. The Morgan is the first true American breed of horse and it has influenced many other breeds of American origin, including the Standard Bred, noted for its speed in harness races.

24 *Below* Scaling muck from a coup cart, *circa* 1910. Coup carts were built with the floor planking laid lengthwise, which made scraping out with a shovel or fork easier. Some farm carts were constructed with tipping bodies.

25 Furniture removal van, *circa* 1910. Although a few small examples were built which could be drawn by a single horse in shafts, most were large vehicles to be pulled by a pair of heavy horses or even a team.

26 *Below* Clarence built by the Gloucester Wagon Works. Drawn by a pair of substantial horses, these town vehicles had seating for four persons inside. A one-horse version with a roof rail for luggage was used for public hire, and nicknamed a 'growler' on account of the noise made by the iron tyres.

27 'Whip behind!' A rare photograph of a coachman using his whip lash to remove street urchins riding on the rear springs of the vehicle. American children played a similar game with sleighs called 'hopping bobs'. Some carriages had a spiked bar across the back to discourage unwelcome passengers.

28 *Opposite above* Harvest carts in the north of England, *circa* 1920. Farm carts were always shod with iron tyres as they wore considerably longer than rubber tyres and were less likely to be pulled off in heavy mud or clay.

29 *Opposite below* Mrs Anne Ashworth driving a Morgan horse stallion to an American road cart. Road carts were originally designed for exercising trotters, although in recent years their use has spread to pleasure driving and some forms of competitive driving.

30 John Coxon, coachman to a Co. Durham doctor, waits outside a patient's house with the horse and gig while his employer makes a visit. *Circa* 1912.

31 *Below* A smart Hackney driven to a butcher's boxcart in a trade turnout class. Butchers favoured fast, flashy horses as speedy deliveries were essential in the days before refrigeration, and an eye catching turnout was a good advertisement.

Mr Peter DuBois driving a Morgan horse
[sta]llion to a Meadowbrook built by the French
[Ca]rriage Co. of Boston. The Meadowbrook is a
[lig]ht, well-sprung vehicle specifically designed for
[dr]iving on tracks and rough ground. Access is
[fro]m the rear via the folding seat, which when
[do]wn traps the driver; hence the generic term
[tr]ap', now indiscriminately used for any two-
[wh]eeled vehicle.

33 *Below* Horse-drawn tanker, *circa* 1900.
Tankers were used for transporting oil, paraffin,
chemicals and water. In very hot dry weather a
type of tanker with a sprinkler at the back was
used in city streets to lay the dust.

Opposite above Phaeton built by Cund & Co. of
ourbridge. The name for these open four-
eeled carriages comes from Greek mythology
en Phaeton, the son of Helios the sun god,
ove his father's sun chariot and the horses
lted, almost setting the world on fire.

36 Mr E. Dickinson's pair of Dales pony mares
driven to a four-wheeled trade lorry in a trade
turnout class. Trade classes are open only to
commercial vehicles including tradesmen's
delivery vehicles, floats, drays, and flat or
Bradford carts.

Opposite below Miss S. Smith driving her pair
Hackney ponies to a modern equirotal phaeton
ring the marathon phase of a combined driving
ent. Equirotal vehicles, built with four equal-
ed wheels and a hinge in the centre of the
dy, were first designed and built in the 1830s.

37 Mr A. Holder's team at the end of the marathon phase of a combined driving event. Marathons are usually divided into five sections which must be driven at a specified pace and within an alloted time, and the course includes natural as well as artificial hazards.

38 *Below* Mrs W. Skill's Hackney driven to a Liverpool gig in a private driving class. During the last century gigs were widely used by bagmen or travelling salesmen who carried their samples in the boot under the seat.

Top American milk wagon built by the ~~Par~~sons Wagon Co. of New York, *circa* 1900. ~~Al~~though these vehicles had a very short front-~~wh~~eel lock, their easy access made them popular ~~wi~~th butchers, bakers, grocers and launderers as ~~we~~ll as milkmen.

40 The author driving a Morgan horse to a Meadowbrook during the presentation phase of a combined driving event in America. The purpose of this phase of the event is to judge the turnout, cleanliness and general condition of the horse, harness and vehicle.

41 Basket *vis-à-vis* phaeton. Basket vehicle bodies were light, inexpensive and easy to maintain, as there was little paintwork to get scratched, and they were favoured by clergymen and others in the lower income bracket.

42 *Below* A competitor negotiates a steep hill during the marathon phase of a driving event. Shoes with studs will give the horse confidence when trotting at speed on slippery roads or down wet or muddy tracks.

Mr George Bowman driving his team through watersplash on the marathon phase of a combined driving event. Usually the watersplash is judged as an artificial hazard, although other fords or streams may be incorporated in the course as natural hazards.

44 Miss Sylvia Brocklebank driving her grey Hackney, Optimistic, to a viceroy, winner of the open harness class at Grantham Show in 1913. Grey Hackneys are very rare and Optimistic's colour was believed to have come from Welsh Mountain pony blood on his dam's side.

45 *Below* Miss Claudia Bunn driving a tandem Welsh ponies to a two-wheeled competition vehicle during the obstacle driving phase of a driving event. The purpose of this section is to test the fitness, obedience and suppleness of the horses after the marathon.

46 A competitor in trouble on the marathon of a combined driving event. Penalties are incurred for putting grooms down, overturning the vehicle, or for any part of the turnout leaving the penalty area surrounding a hazard before completing the hazard correctly.

47 *Below* Mr George Bowman driving his team of Lippizaners to a modern competition vehicle. The Lippizaner breed dates back to the mid 1500s and they make excellent carriage horses, incorporating the qualities of elegance and style with an amenable temperament.

48 Brougham built by Tucker & Co. of London. Small two-seater versions of this popular vehicle were favoured by doctors and subsequently known as 'pill-boxes' on account of their size and medical connections.

49 *Below* Mr Emil Jung driving a team of Holsteiners to a modern Daresbury phaeton. The demands of modern competitive driving have resulted in the designing and manufacture of a whole new range of carriages incorporating the use of new materials and technology.

50 An experimental improved knifeboard
omnibus introduced by the London Road Car
Co. in April 1881, with a front entrance and
improved roof access. The front entrance proved
unsatisfactory but the other features were used in
later models with success.

51 *Below* Mr Keith Farnhill driving his team to a
modern Presteigne dogcart. Fifty years ago it was
extremely difficult to find anyone who could
repair horse-drawn vehicles; now there are nearly
twenty firms engaged solely in the manufacture of
carriages in England alone.

Opposite above Mr W. Moorhouse driving a
Welsh pony to a ralli car in a private driving
class. Ralli cars were named after the Greek
Ralipping family from Surrey and may be either
two- or four-wheeled, although the latter are also
known as curve-panel phaetons.

54 Mr Mark Broadbent driving a team of Welsh
ponies to a modern Fenix competition vehicle. In
recent years the use of new materials, including
epoxy resins and fibreglass has been
experimented with in the development of strong
but light competition carriages.

Opposite below Wagonette built by Hooper of
London. Hoopers were one of the most famous of
the London coach builders and supplied many
superb vehicles to the royal family as well as the
nobility and heads of state of other European
countries.

55 HRH The Duke of Edinburgh receiving the winner's trophy at a combined driving event. The carriage is a Bennington phaeton, a modern vehicle combining traditional looks with new technology including all-metal wheels and shock absorbers as part of the suspension.

56 *Opposite above* The artificial hazards on the marathon of a combined driving event are designed to test the skill of the driver and the obedience and manoeuvrability of the horses. Unexpected accidents often occur when driving through these hazards at speed.

57 *Opposite below* Australian pony jinker. These well-sprung vehicles were ideally suited to the unmade roads and rough ground of country districts and the long shafts were intended to give a smoother ride. The name is believed to have derived originally from 'jingle', a term used in the West Country for a trap.

58 Mrs D. McDonald driving a pair of Australian ponies to a Whitechapel buggy built by Messrs Curry & Sons of Victoria. Many American vehicles were imported into Australia during the second half of the nineteenth century and the American influence can be clearly seen in subsequent Australian-built carriages.

59 *Below* Australian Sydney sulky. These vehicles were built to order by a firm called Stocks & O'Neill of Sydney and were beautifully finished with leather upholstery and lavish brass fittings, including a brass foot-bell just visible underneath the vehicle.

horses were often temporarily quietened with excessive hard work, abusive treatment or even dope, and many placid horses were bought from the dealers' yards only to be returned a week or two later as wild as tigers. Lameness could be temporarily cured by wrapping the leg in wet cotton or by laming the unfortunate horse in the other leg so as to restore the balance and make it appear sound. Old horses could be made to look younger by fattening them up with flaked maize, boiled barley or linseed gruel, and another trick was to disguise the hollows above the eyes of old horses by carefully inserting a straw through a tiny hole cut into the skin and literally blowing the hollow up like a balloon. Wise buyers checked the horses' teeth for age, but even here they could still be deceived, for the sly copers had a method of replacing the black marks which all horses under ten years of age have on the crown of their incisor teeth but which disappear after that age. The coper could burn these marks on to the teeth with a hot iron, and they did it with such skill that the results could easily be taken as genuine. Scars, including broken knees, could be disguised behind a layer of dye craftily applied with a cloth, and broken-winded horses were starved of hay and water the day before the customer came to see them, as this treatment could temporarily improve their condition. Most horse dealers kept a private store of remedies made up from such bizarre ingredients as burnt cork, best butter, soot, soft soap and nutmeg, which they used to cure such ailments as the cough, colic and inflammation of the tendons.

The English dealers bought their horses from a variety of sources, depending upon the use for which they were intended. A great many horses for work in omnibuses and carriers' vans came from Ireland and were shipped over in consignments by the big Dublin dealers, but the best carriage horses came from Yorkshire and were predominantly Cleveland Bay, Yorkshire Coach Horse, Hackney, or a combination of all three. Norfolk also produced many fine horses. Dealers' agents all over Europe visited the regular sales on the lookout for likely horses, and made it their business to know all the breeders and farmers who occasionally bred a good horse or two. Foreigners were not blind to the value of the English carriage horse, and began to buy large numbers of mares, which were considered inferior to geldings for carriage work because of their temperament and were consequently cheaper. This short-sighted policy had a disastrous effect, for the Continental buyers used their imported mares for breeding when they came out of harness, while the English were eventually left with no breeding stock and had to begin importing carriage horses from the Continent again. Mr J. East, giving evidence before the select committee of the House of Lords on the subject of horses in 1873, said that the French agents 'buy the very best and they get mares; you cannot get them to buy a bad mare'. Sir Walter Gilbey, in *The Harness Horse*, 1898, stated that the Continental buyers 'did not confine their purchases to any particular breed of mares; roomy hunting mares and mares of that class were eagerly purchased to cross with Hackney sires'. Speaking of the results of this breeding policy, Gilbey added, 'English dealers who make a speciality of horses for harness and general road use go abroad in search of the animals they require, knowing perfectly well that upstanding carriage horses, possessed of shape and action, are to be found in the breeding centres of the Continent.' Between 1863 and 1872 over twenty-nine thousand horses were imported into England; between 1883 and 1892 the figure was nearer one hundred and forty-six thousand, and this included horses from France, Holland, Italy, Germany and Hungary, although people still continued to believe that they did not possess the stamina of the English breeds.

Wherever they originated from, the horses were not generally bought by the dealers until they were four-year-olds and mature enough to begin serious work. Many of the Continental horses had been broken in as two-year-olds by their breeders and used for light farm work, but they had to be accustomed to the sights and sounds of the cities in which they were to work. Others were completely untouched and had to be trained from scratch. The usual method of breaking them in was to harness them alongside an older experienced horse in a skeleton break – a light four-wheeled vehicle with a high boxseat specially designed for this purpose – and take them out into the streets. It took about eight months to have them fully trained. In Victorian times, London's Piccadilly was often crowded with dealers' nagsmen training young horses, and one old nagsman with considerable experience on the subject insisted that the safest place to put a young horse in harness was in a crowded street where it would be too distracted by all the activity around it to try and kick its way out of the vehicle. Only when the young horse was resigned to its work and safe to drive would it be offered for sale.

Auctions were at the centre of the horse trade and they brought together the inevitable collection of characters – copers, strappers, corn chandlers, retired coachmen, bus drivers, grooms, farmers and gentlemen. In London the biggest repository was Tattersalls, which in 1865 moved from Grosvenor Place to Knightsbridge where they had built a palatial glass-domed covered yard, costing thirty thousand pounds, in which they held sales every Monday throughout the year and also on Thursdays 'during the season'. They specialized in quality carriage horses and vehicles, while other sales like Rymills in the Barbican and Aldridges in St Martin's Lane dealt mainly with draught horses, and every Friday the Islington Cattle Market was the venue for the weekly donkey sale, where three thousand of these animals changed hands annually.

Chapter 5
The private carriage

Private carriages, as distinct from public or commercial vehicles, can be divided into two quite separate types; those in which the passengers drove themselves and those in which they were driven by a coachman. The first private vehicles were always coachman-driven, as it was considered a lowly occupation to drive, but when driving came to be regarded as a sport rather than as a means of conveyance the situation altered and many notable personalities including the Prince of Wales, later George IV, and his fashionable friends, took to keeping a carriage and pair. A gentleman's skill with the reins even came to be regarded as a measure of his social status.

The first private vehicles were the town coaches which traced their origins to the crudely built vehicles of the sixteenth century, and which were so heavy that it took teams of four or even six stoutly built horses to pull them. Apart from their excessive weight, they were ungainly, difficult to manoeuvre and very uncomfortable. Around 1790, when driving started to be looked upon as a leisure activity suitable for young gentlemen, a variety of light sporty vehicles made their appearance, most notably the first phaetons, which soon became very popular and were produced in large numbers. The name 'phaeton' denoted a four-wheel owner-driven vehicle seating two or more persons, and was derived from Phaeton, the son of Helios the sun god, who according to Greek mythology stole his father's sun chariot and proceeded to lose control of the horses which bolted towards the earth and nearly set it on fire. A possible explanation of why these vehicles were so named could be that young Regency men about town were as reckless in their driving as Phaeton had been in his. The early phaetons were extremely high, with the light double seat suspended from whip springs above an undercarriage that, according to Felton, writing in 1794, could take the form of a traditional stout wooden perch or a pair of iron perches curved into a loop shape under which the front axle turned to allow a full lock. The front wheels were about four feet high, the rear wheels six feet, although instances of even larger wheels were occasionally recorded. On account of their height these phaetons were very dangerous to drive, although this element was said to have added to the pleasure of those who drove them. They became known as 'highflyers' or 'high perch' phaetons, while those with twin iron perches were colloquially known as 'crane necks'. The first phaetons were drawn by pairs of fast horses but later versions were drawn by four or sometimes six horses, and when this was the case the leaders were postillion-driven and only the wheelers or back pair of horses driven from the boxseat. In order to eliminate the risks which could have resulted should the postillion have fallen off, some phaetons had an ingenious emergency device operated from the boxseat which opened the hook at the end of the pole and released the lead horses.

The first gigs were built around 1780 and were simple two-wheeled vehicles seating two persons and drawn by one horse, although in later times it became quite usual to drive two horses tandem fashion (one in front of the other) to a gig. Some gigs were very roughly built, with the seat little more than a plank and without even the refinement of a cushion, and in England if they cost less than twelve pounds to purchase and had the words 'taxed cart' painted on them they were subject to a tax of only twelve shillings a year. Other more stylish gigs, in common with all other two-wheeled vehicles, were obliged to pay the standard tax of three pounds, seventeen shillings a year. Gigs were used mainly by businessmen or commercial travellers who could use the boot under the seat for storing their samples, but a lady never travelled in a gig unless she wanted to earn herself a reputation for being 'fast'. Some British jobmasters made a speciality of hiring out gigs when the government levied a tax on all carriages for sale, although this was soon repealed. Many types of gigs were built to meet specific demands, including rib-chair, polo, chair-back and skeleton gigs, but one of the most distinctive was the suicide gig, so named because the groom had a separate seat to himself which was built three feet higher than the already high driver's seat. The ease with which one of these gigs could be turned over made it one of the most dangerous of all vehicles. During the nineteenth century, when the gig became an eminently suitable vehicle for businessmen who commuted into the city from the suburbs, many further designs were introduced to cater for particular preferences and purposes. The Honourable Fitzroy Stanhope designed the gig which now bears his name and which resembled the old type of unsprung rib-chair gig but with the addition of four springs which made it very smooth to ride in, although rather heavy. Tilbury, the London coachbuilder, was responsible for another type of gig, the Tilbury gig, which was light and elegant but unsuitable for 'bagmen' or commercial travellers as it had no boot. Liverpool gigs, many of them built by the famous coach builders, Lawton of London and Liverpool, became very popular on account of their stylish shape, and other notable types included round-back, spindle-back, well-bottom and dennett gigs. A few gigs were fitted with leather hoods to afford some protection for the passengers, and they were sometimes called 'buggies', although this term was later adopted by the Americans and used indiscriminately to describe many types of two- or four-wheeled vehicles. The ornately carved chaises used on the Continent were another branch of the gig family.

Some early gigs were specially designed for the trotting matches which were popular at the time and these were built with very large wheels and a high seat for one person, which earned them the name of 'sulkies'. Another offshoot of the gig was the whisky, a very light cane-bodied vehicle to be drawn by one horse. Its name came from the fact that these speedy little gigs 'whisked' along the ground at a great pace.

The dogcart was directly derived from the gig and it became one of the most popular vehicles because of its versatility. Early examples had two wheels but differed from gigs in that they carried four people instead of two, the double seats being arranged back to back with the tailboard letting down on chains to provide a footrest for the rear passengers. Their deep boots had slatted sides for ventilation and were used to carry sporting dogs; hence their name. Four-wheeled dogcarts were favoured on country estates for general use: running messages, collecting luggage, transporting the family to church or the owner to market, and could be drawn by one horse or, if the shafts were removed and a pole and splinter bar substituted, a pair or a team. The cocking cart, first built around 1800, was a form of dogcart with a large boot for transporting fighting cocks to mains or fights, and the wide range of other carts included country carts, Essex carts, panel carts and many others built for use mainly in rural areas.

For those who found driving a highflyer a little disconcerting, the curricle, first designed and built around 1800, often provided the answer. The low, elegant body was hung on side-springs with cee-springs at the rear, and was fitted with a hood and a rumble seat at the back on which the groom sat. The curricle was unique among two-wheeled vehicles, as it was the only one specifically built to be drawn by a pair, the harness being specially made with a steel bar which went across the horses' backs and supported the pole. Curricle horses commanded high prices, as they had to match perfectly in action as well as size and colour, especially when the curricle became a fashionable vehicle and was patronized by such prestigious owners as the Prince of Wales, the flamboyant Count d'Orsay, and Charles Dickens, who is said to have spent all the money he received from the publication of the Pickwick Papers in 1837 on such a vehicle. The most unforgettable curricle of all time was that owned by the wealthy actor, 'Romeo' Coates, and described as being like a classic sea-god's car in shape. The body was of polished copper encrusted with sea-shells and frequent repetitions of the owner's crest, a crowing cock, with the motto 'While I live, I'll crow.' Drawn by a pair of white horses, the equipage was regularly seen in Hyde Park in London driven by 'Romeo', who was often followed by a pack of urchins shouting, 'Cock-a-doodle-do, cock-a-doodle-do.'

The cabriolet, which resembled the curricle in many respects except that it was built for a single horse and not a pair, superseded the curricle as a fashionable vehicle, as it was equally impressive in appearance but cheaper to maintain. Instead of having a groom's seat at the back, there was a platform on which stood a diminutive groom, nicknamed a 'tiger' on account of his striped black and yellow waistcoat. 'Tigers' had to be very small in order to emphasize the size and substance of the magnificent carriage horse. Like its predecessor, the cabriolet had many devotees, who found it an ideal vehicle for going out at night, and in order to warn road users of the vehicle's approach at speed in the darkness, the horse often wore a small bell attached to its collar.

In 1824, the first of a whole new range of phaetons was built – a particularly low-slung pony vehicle produced for George IV, who was beginning to feel too old and stiff for the more daring vehicles of his youth. The vehicle was built by William Cook, the royal coachbuilder, and its wheels measured twenty-one inches in front and thirty-three inches at the back. The dashboard curved up over the pony's hindquarters in a graceful line and the low body allowed for easy access. The new phaeton aroused such interest that in 1828 Princess Victoria had one built for her own use which was drawn by a team of postillion-driven ponies, and many other ladies followed her example until the pony phaeton became a necessity for any lady with social aspirations. Beautifully attired in the latest fashion, she would drive her phaeton with a groom either seated on the rumble or, occasionally, riding behind at a discreet distance, and in her hand she would carry a light but practically useless parasol whip. The groom was always dressed in immaculate livery and was there more for his part in the conspicuous display than for his value as a servant.

In 1828 the mail phaeton, a substantial vehicle with a hooded boxseat and a railed seat behind for use by grooms, found favour among gentlemen who used it both for pleasure driving and for posting, as it had plenty of room for luggage. Like the mail coaches from which it took its name, it had a perch, and the whole equipage was given a coaching flavour by the use of heavy coach horses to pull it and such accessories as chains instead of pole straps. The mail phaeton was invariably a dark colour; bottle green, navy or black, and never lined as this was thought to detract from its character as essentially a man's vehicle. Demi-mail phaetons differed from mail phaetons in that they had no perch, being hung on elliptic springs, and were consequently much lighter. Stanhope phaetons had the further refinement of a spindled seat and, being even lighter, could be drawn by one horse only. Although these new designs were originally brought out by particular coach builders, if they proved popular other builders would be quick to copy them and many slightly different versions of the same vehicle would appear. The T-cart was simply a small version of the Stanhope phaeton with the groom's seat reduced in size so that it sat only one, whereas the Beaufort phaeton was like a mail phaeton but with an extra seat incorporated so that shooting parties of six persons could be accommodated.

The most elegant of all the phaetons was the spider phaeton, which combined the qualities of lightness and elegance to perfection and was acknowledged to be the ideal vehicle in which to display the shape and action of fine carriage horses. The body consisted of a hooded seat set upon a pair of arched irons, which supported a small platform at the back on which a removable groom's seat was positioned.

Towards the end of the nineteenth century two new designs of vehicles made their debut. The first was the ralli car, which was named after the Greek shipping family of that name who lived in Surrey, and it could be built with either two or four wheels. It resembled the dogcart in the style of seating but was distinguishable by having the shafts inside rather than under or alongside the body, and it also had side panels which curved out over the wheels to form mudguards.

The governess car was almost invariably two-wheeled, although a few four-wheeled versions were also built. The low circular or square body had seats on either side and was entered by a door at the back, and it was drawn by one horse or pony, which had to be quiet, as the design of the body did not make it especially comfortable to drive. It was ideal for children, as they could not fall out easily, and the handle was situated halfway down the outside of the door well out of the reach of small hands. Before governess cars were introduced, low pony phaetons with strong basketwork bodies to stand up to the abuse they received from children were generally used by governesses when they took their charges out for an airing in the park. Although governess cars were essentially country vehicles, many fine examples with elegant spindle-sided bodies were turned out by the city coach builders. Plainer solid-sided governess cars were often referred to as 'tub' traps, by way of reference to their overall shape.

For those travelling in towns, but not owning their own town coach, a service of sorts was provided by the hackney coaches, but those travelling longer distances across country normally used one of two methods; the post-chaise system or their own private travelling chariot. The private travelling chariot was designed with the primary purposes of being a safe and comfortable conveyance in which to embark upon a long journey like the fashionable grand tour of Europe. There were luggage platforms at both the front and the back. When fully loaded they could be extremely heavy, but this was of little consequence as four or six horses were used to pull it. The postillion riders, and also the footmen who rode on a seat between the rear springs, were employees of the chariot's owner. Some travelling chariots were ingeniously fitted out, like the one used by Lord Vernon which Charles Dickens encountered in Switzerland in 1846 and described as 'an extraordinary carriage, where you touch a spring and a chair flies out, touch another spring and a bed appears, touch another spring and a closet of pickles opens, touch another spring and disclose a pantry'. (Quoted in J. Forster, *The Life of Charles Dickens*, 1873.) Travelling chariots were built by a number of the top coach builders, and according to Sir Walter Gilbey, 'in the year 1841, the business of Messrs Adams and Hooper was almost entirely confined to the manufacture of the most complete and expensive travelling carriages for members of the English royal family and the great nobles of England and continental Europe'. Some were fitted with interior lights, venetian blinds in case the sun was hot, integral sword cases and hatboxes, and one built for the Earl of Winchelsea in 1825 'was constructed with the box under the driving seat open to the interior of the vehicle, so that there was ample length for the traveller to lie down and sleep while on his journey'. A number of other vehicles were also specially designed for long journeys, including the dormeuse, the fourgon – used for transporting servants and luggage – and the britchka, an example of which was built for the Honourable Leicester Stanhope and which 'by the movement of different parts of the body forms an agreeable open carriage by day, and a convenient bedchamber by night'. (Sir W. Gilbey, *Modern Carriages*, 1898.)

Even for the less adventurous, a carriage was an outward sign of rank, wealth and privilege, and it was the aim of every middle-class family to own one. Aristocrats needed a carriage house stocked with a variety of vehicles for both pleasure and business, and the imaginative carriage designers gave them plenty of choice. One of the most useful was the landau, which originated in the West German fortress town of that name around 1790 and was introduced into England about ten years later. The first landaus were built on a perch undercarriage, but later examples had elliptic springs and were much lighter as a result. The twin hoods, which were a characteristic of the landau, could be raised in wet weather to form a closed carriage or lowered when it was fair, making this an adaptable vehicle, and it was entered by means of a door on either side of the body, the glazed top part of which could be lowered into the door panel when the hoods were down. The Earl of Sefton had a canoe-shaped landau built by his coachbuilders, Messrs Hooper, and this form of landau became known as the Sefton landau, while a more angular form designed by the Earl of Shelburne came to bear his name. At one of the carriage exhibitions held in 1862 it was reported that 'in consequence of the many improvements effected in the manufacture of landaus, the chief of which is the great reduction in weight, the demand for them has already increased', and towards the end of the eighteenth century it was claimed that, 'No carriage has been improved upon to such an extent in twenty years as the landau.' So popular did this carriage become on account of its versatility that most private establishments of any importance had one, and Thrupp, the famous coach builder, once said that in contrasting the numbers of different types of vehicles, 'I find that the landau has become the favourite carriage.' Several versions of the landau were built, including formal state landaus, which were postillion-driven, and a number of these ornate vehicles are still in regular use at the Royal Mews in London.

The victoria became enormously popular after the Prince of Wales brought one to London from Paris in 1869, and it became the perfect vehicle for fashionable ladies to go out for a drive in, as the open sides of the body provided an ideal showcase for the fashions of the day. The name, with its royal connotations, also appealed to the snobbery of middle-class society.

In design, it resembled a hooded pony phaeton but with the addition of a boxseat for the coachman, and it could be drawn by one or two horses. The victoria was a summer vehicle, much used during the so-called 'season' which ran from Easter to July, but for winter use or if the weather was inclement a brougham (pronounced 'broam') would be used. The vehicle was named after its designer, Lord Brougham, who wanted a light handy carriage for town use but with more comfort and better visibility than a closed cab. Lord Brougham first approached the firm of Sharp and Bland, but they did not seem keen to undertake the commission to build the first brougham, so he went to a neighbouring firm of coach builders, Messrs Robinson and Cook, who on 18 May 1838 produced the first brougham. It was an immediate success, and these neat enclosed vehicles seating two or four persons inside and having a boxseat at the front for the coachman became increasingly numerous. They were especially popular with the medical profession, and as a result they became affectionately known as 'pill boxes'. The larger four-seater version called the double brougham was usually drawn by a pair of horses.

The barouche originated in France around 1800 and it was a large and impressive vehicle requiring two or four big quality horses to pull it, although on formal occasions six might be used, either driven from the boxseat or postillion-driven. The body was semi-enclosed by one hood and was suspended from cee-springs with a seat or platform at the back for grooms or footmen. In the absence of either, a spiked bar was fitted to the rear of the vehicle to prevent street urchins from riding on the back unseen by the coachman or occupants. On some vehicles the groom had to stand on the undersprings, which jolted so much that one eminent writer claimed they caused grooms 'to spit blood from violent and continued concussion'. Being an expensive vehicle both to buy and to maintain, only the wealthiest could afford to turn one out in the correct style, and in his essay on 'Modern Carriages', written in 1888, Hooper states that 'the depression of agriculture in England and Ireland, affecting all trades and manufactures, affected the coach building industry, and more especially checked the building of barouches'.

According to Sir Walter Gilbey, writing in 1905, 'the wagonette is said to have been introduced into this country in the year 1845 by the late Prince Consort', and a writer in the *Coachbuilders', Harness Makers' and Saddlers' Art Journal* of 1885 stated that it was 'a perfect open family carriage'. Wagonettes always had four wheels and were invariably built on elliptic springs. The body was fitted with seats on both sides which faced inwards and were reached by a rear door as with a governess car, and there was a raised boxseat for the driver. A number of variations on the basic theme were produced, including the Portland wagonette designed by the Duke of Portland in 1893, which had a folding hood, the Lonsdale wagonette designed by the Earl of Lonsdale, which had twin hoods which folded back over the wheels but could be raised to form a closed carriage, and another form designed by Mr Neil of Bath with an unusual wood-and-glass 'head' or top.

With large numbers of horses continually being broken in for harness work, an essential vehicle was the break which, as its name implies, was originally used for the training of young driving horses. The skeleton break, which was used specifically for this purpose, was a light four-wheeled vehicle with a high boxseat out of reach of kicking hooves and a platform behind on which stood a groom who could jump down to lend assistance if the need arose. The name was also used for one or two other vehicles, including the wagonette-break, which was a much larger and sturdier form of the wagonette, and the body break, which closely resembled it, having a longer body which could accommodate up to twenty passengers. Some large households and schools used body breaks for conveying the staff and pupils to church on a Sunday, and jobmasters often used them or charabancs for staff outings.

In countries where snow prevented the use of wheeled vehicles in winter, sleighs were used, and many fine examples were built, especially in North America and in Russia where sleighs operated as taxis in the larger towns and cities. American designers and builders were also responsible for a distinctive range of light two- and four-wheeled vehicles with such names as piano-top buggies and triple buckboards, suitable for use on the rough unmade roads which connected towns and settlements in rural areas. Some, like the four-wheeled surrey, had detachable tops to shade the passengers, but other more utilitarian buggies were often unsprung except for the driver's seat, which was set upon elliptic springs at each end. The Duke of Beaufort, in a work entitled *Driving* of 1889, said of American vehicles, 'There seems happily to be little danger of the introduction into England of any of these curiously ungraceful vehicles.' Because of similarities in the terrain, many American designs were copied by Australian builders or modified to suit their requirements, with the result that Australia has few vehicles of original design, even the Australian jinker being a variation on an American road cart. South Africa, on the other hand, has the capecart, a robust two-wheeled vehicle with a cover to shade the occupants and drawn by a pair of horses or oxen harnessed with special 'cape' harness, and in India a similar form of harnessing was sometimes used to enable two animals to be harnessed to their national vehicle, the two-wheeled tonga. Usually tongas were drawn by only one animal, although Lord Baden-Powell in his book *Indian Memories* described seeing a tonga with one pony between the shafts and another harnessed alongside it in what he called 'Hungarian' fashion.

It would be impossible to mention all the different varieties of vehicles likely to be found in a private coach house, for as James Paton wrote in 1875, 'The forms of carriages as now built are so numerous as almost to defy classification, and they altogether baffle detailed description.' Many, like the sociable, town chariot and private drag, were adapted from established types, while others were the unsuccessful whim of wealthy, imaginative but talentless owner–designers, of which the upper social strata produced a great many. The best-designed vehicles stood the test of time and were still in use at the beginning of the twentieth century; the rest just disappeared and are only remembered from old prints or coach builders' plans.

Chapter 6
Public transport

Before the stage-coach system got under way in Europe, and even afterwards for those who liked privacy and felt disinclined to share a stuffy coach with strangers, the only way to travel on long journeys, unless you were wealthy enough to own a private travelling chariot, was by post chaise. The post chaises were not unlike small coaches with the front section cut away to leave a light enclosed body seating two people and entered by half-glass doors on either side. A platform at the rear of the vehicle was used to carry luggage, including the massive travelling trunks or 'imperials' as they were sometimes called, and the colloquial name of 'yellow bounders' by which these vehicles were known in England is believed to be attributable to the colour they were always painted and the way in which the whip- or cee-springs from which the body was suspended caused the vehicle to bounce. Occasionally these vehicles were driven from a boxseat but it was more usual for them to be postillion-driven by postboys (some of them quite old), who rode the nearside horse and wore an iron guard strapped to their right leg to prevent it from being crushed between the horse they were riding and the pole. The post chaises were owned by innkeepers, who hired them out complete with horses and postboys – one if two horses were being used, two if four horses were being used. Every ten to fifteen miles the horses and postboys were changed at a posting inn in much the same fashion as the mail coaches were horsed. Post chaise was not a cheap way to travel, although it was reasonably quick, and travellers expected to pay one shilling and sixpence a mile, all inclusive, for this service if two horses were used, and three shillings a mile if four horses were used. Some post chaises were specially built for the purpose but many were the discarded travelling chariots of gentlemen. As William Pyne wrote in his *Microcosm* of 1804, 'a post-chaise and four, which is travelling in its best style, will go ten miles at an average, as they keep running on without any diminution of their pace even up rising ground, except these be uncommonly steep'.

The Duke of Beaufort spoke highly in *Driving*, 1889, of the French posting system, which was fast and efficient, and went on to add that, 'In Italy in many parts the travelling was excellent by post; always two boys to four horses, and they drove really fast and well.' An efficient but slower system was also operated in Germany.

In towns the choice of public transport was wider, with cabs of both the two- and four-wheeled variety vying for trade with horse-drawn omnibuses and, later, trams. Even in Victorian times, a few hackney coaches were still to be seen in the cities, discarded relics of a gentleman's coach house demoted to standing at cab ranks or street kerbs, the horses 'like the tattered remnants of a forgotten cavalry charge'. A contributor to the *London Magazine* in 1825 asked, 'Who can be a gentleman and visit in a hackney coach? Who can, indeed? to predicate nothing of stinking straw and broken windows, and cushions on which the last dandy has cleaned his shoes, and of the last fever it has carried to Guy's, or the last load of convicts transported to the hulks.' They served their purpose but left much to be desired, and around 1805 the first light two-wheeled cabs were introduced into England from the Continent, but they too had many faults and it was not until 1823 that a coach builder from Albany Street in London, Mr David Davies, put the first licensed hackney cabs on the roads. The name 'cab' was derived from the cabriolet which they resembled in many respects, except that the driver had a seat to himself which was positioned between the body and the wheel. Dickens mentions in *Pickwick Papers* a scene where three people were 'squeezed into a hackney cabriolet, the driver sitting in his own particular little dickey at the side'. The hood could be raised or lowered to suit the passengers and there was a heavy waterproof apron which could be drawn across the front to protect the passengers from rain or dirt thrown up from the road. Seven years later an even more unusual vehicle made its appearance; it owed its name of the 'coffin cab' to the fact that the hood had been replaced by a high rectangular box, unpleasantly like a coffin, which was perhaps why it never became popular. In a trade manual Mr Hooper, the coach builder, described this bizarre vehicle as 'a light two-wheeled cab with a fixed panel top and carrying two persons inside . . . the driver sat on a little seat over the off-side wheel. These carriages hung high and were dangerous if the horse fell, but they prepared the public for a faster, less cumbersome and less costly vehicle than the old coaches.' Enterprising designers were quick to bring out an interesting selection of 'patent' cabs, including some with back doors like the Bulnois cab, some with the driver on the roof, and even one with three wheels, but it was not until 1834 that Mr J.A. Hansom, an architect, produced his version, which he drove from Leicestershire to London as proof of its roadworthiness. It was a square ugly structure with short axles projecting from the sides of the body. The driver sat at the front of the roof, and it is said that the two wheels were seven feet six inches in height. The passengers got in through two doors on either side at the front. On arrival in London, Hansom received a startling offer of £10,000 from a firm who wanted to build and market his design but before the contract was signed certain faults in the vehicle were discovered and the money was never paid over. Within two years the secretary of the Safety

Cabriolet and Two Wheeled Carriage Co., Mr J. Chapman, had amended Hansom's basic design to eradicate the faults, and he sold his patent back to Hansom, whose name the cab now bears. His amendments including placing the driver's seat at the back of the cab and level with the roof, and putting the axle underneath the body. Fifty cabs were built to this design, and they became an immediate success, especially as they had a reputation for being a safe means of transport. To avoid any possible confusion, they all had the words 'Hansom's Patent Safety' painted on the sides. According to Sir Walter Gilbey, an authority on carriages, 'the safety element consisted in such an arrangement of the framework that the cab would not upset if tilted up or down'. Unfortunately, rival firms soon copied the design, but added the word 'not' in tiny letters in front of 'Hansom's Patent Safety', in a vain attempt to avoid the lawsuits which inevitably followed.

Variations of the hansom cab soon appeared in many European capitals, as well as in some of the cities of Australia and the east coast of America. Over a period of time, further slight amendments were made to Hansom's design, including making the windows larger, cutting away the body under the seat so that the axle could go straight across instead of being cranked, and fitting half-doors in place of the leather apron at the front. Several notable firms contributed to the amenities of the vehicle, including Evans of Liverpool, Marston of Birmingham and, most notably, Forders of Wolverhampton who became the most famous hansom-cab builders of all time. The Society of Arts, who had been making awards for developments in carriage building for over a hundred years, offered a prize for the best two-wheeled public conveyance in 1873 and Forders won it with one of their superb hansom cabs, which was described as 'marking a new era in street vehicles'. As Sir Walter Gilbey wrote, 'Forders' hansom showed how the weight of a cab could be reduced by the use of better material and workmanship.' Among the many refinements which Forders introduced to their cabs was an apparatus which enabled the driver to open and shut the doors at the front by means of a lever operated from his rooftop seat. Other builders soon copied the idea, including the Arlington Cab Co. of Regent Street, London, whose patent cab was immodestly advertised as 'the latest, most handsome, roomy, convenient and best finished hansom cab on the market'. In 1880 the Forder cab had reached the pinnacle of perfection and their elegant hansoms with rubber-tyred wheels were beautifully fitted out inside with luxurious upholstery, ashtrays, looking-glasses and a bell to attract the driver's attention. Instead of straw on the floor as in the old hackney coaches, there was fitted rubber matting, and the windows had silk blinds for the benefit of passengers seeking privacy or shade.

A number of English noblemen, including the Earl of Lonsdale and Lord Shrewsbury, joined the ranks of cab proprietors and proceeded to set the same high standards of turnout that they expected with their own private carriages. Lord Shrewsbury was the first proprietor to introduce rubber tyres on his cabs, which were always spotlessly clean and driven by a smart and polite cabbie, a sharp contrast to the hackney coaches and abusive drivers of earlier times. The horses were well cared for and fast, many being ex-racehorses which had proved too slow for the racetrack. In spite of their position at the back of the vehicle which prevented them from seeing anything more of the horse than his ears, the cabbies were extremely skilful drivers who could gauge distances and gaps between other vehicles with alarming precision. Most of the cabbies hired their hansoms and horses from small proprietors who owned four or five and hired them out by the day or night. The usual daily charge was about a pound or twenty-five shillings during the season and fifteen shillings for other times of the year. The hansom cab or 'gondola of London' was considered to be a rather dashing vehicle and a lady would never have been seen in one. Elderly people found them too fast and daring, and some passengers complained that they were too small to accommodate their baggage. To suit these parties, the four-wheeled cab was introduced by Mr David Davies, the man who had earlier been responsible for bringing the first two-wheeled hackney cabs to London. Known as 'covered cabs', they carried two passengers inside and one on the boxseat beside the driver, and it is said that Lord Brougham took the idea for the vehicle which bears his name from these. Later versions accommodated four persons inside, and were called 'growlers' on account of the deafening noise their iron-tyred wheels made on the stone or macadam roads. Some growlers, or 'Clarences', as they were correctly called, became as decrepit as the old hackney coaches in time, and the condition of the wretched animals which drew them became a constant source of concern for the 'mercy patrols' of the Royal Society for the Prevention of Cruelty to Animals, which visited the cab ranks regularly. It was not unusual for a cab horse to have done fifty or more miles in a night. An Act of Parliament passed in 1838 compelled all cab drivers to take out a licence and wear a badge, but it did nothing to ensure that the cabs and horses were properly maintained.

In Ireland, the place of the cab was taken by the jaunting car or 'outside car', as they were sometimes known. These traditional two-wheelers had two rows of back-to-back seats on which the passengers sat facing the road on each side, their luggage being stored in a lidded well between the seats. Hinged footrests, which could be folded up when the seats were not in use, let down and hung over the outsides of the wheels, and the driver or 'jarvey' drove from a little seat at the front or from one of the side seats. Although found all over Ireland, these distinctive vehicles were never used with any success elsewhere. Coach proprietors like Purcell and Co. of Dublin operated mail- and stage-coach services in many parts of the country, and transport between the main coaching roads and in isolated areas was provided by Bianconi cars, which were the brainchild of an Italian immigrant, Carlo Bianconi. 'Bians', as they were locally known, were either two- or four-wheeled back-to-back vehicles rather like large jaunting cars, seating up to twenty persons and drawn by up to four horses. So successful were Bianconi's passenger vehicles that by 1825 they covered 1,000 miles of road every day.

Omnibuses of a sort were first used in Paris as early as 1662, but their popularity was short-lived, and it was not until 1819 that Monsieur Jacques Lafitte revived the idea. He commissioned George Shillibeer, an ex-naval man who had gone to Paris to set himself up as a coach builder, to produce an improved version, and the success it brought Lafitte encouraged Shillibeer to try running an omnibus service in London. On 4 July 1829 the first omnibus in London ran between Paddington Green and The Bank, and the idea soon caught on, until by 1904 there were one thousand four hundred omnibuses in London alone. Shillibeer's bus set the pattern for all the others, and was described as a large vehicle with twenty-two inside seats, drawn by three strong upstanding bay horses. His men dressed in velvet suits and were extremely polite to passengers, and the buses were equipped with books and magazines to prevent the passengers from becoming bored on long journeys. As different omnibus companies set up in business, it became accepted practice for the buses to be painted with the colours which depicted their line, such as dark green for Bayswater and white for Putney. In 1850, a new design of omnibus called the 'knifeboard' was introduced, and was unique in that it was the first to carry passengers on the roof. In *Bygones*, 1948, Dick Hunt, the Hove jobmaster, recalled the knifeboard horse bus of his youth:

> A compactly built, boxy looking vehicle, rounded at the corners, front and back, three square windows on each side and set above the coloured body, a steepish step up took you inside the door, placed at the end of the bus. Another step up to the near side was the 'monkey board' on which the conductor stood. A long strap fixed to the bus behind his shoulder gave him something to hang on to and at the same time helped him to drop from his round step to the ground, also providing him with something to hit the side of the bus with when he wanted to signal his mate to 'go on'. The roof was oval, with a long seat extending from the door to the coachman's back, the passengers sitting back to back in two rows facing either side; a little footboard was provided for one's feet which enabled the passenger to stretch his legs straight out towards the advertisement boards. The coachman's box was placed between two others provided for the use of travellers. A powerful footbrake was installed handy to the driver's right foot.

The new design was well received by passengers, who appreciated the excellent view they got as they looked down on to the pavements. In hot weather, the roof seats were much pleasanter than the cramped inside seats. At a later date it was found necessary to fit two long boards to the sides of the roof, to prevent people on the pavement looking up and catching a glimpse of the ankles of lady passengers. When the publicity potential of omnibuses was realized, these 'modesty boards', as they were called, became emblazoned with advertisements and brought the bus proprietors a little extra income. An even later design of omnibus, the 'garden seat' omnibus, had a double row of seats in pairs, one behind the other and all facing the front, and this type became so popular that it soon ousted the other forms.

The ideal sort of bus horse, according to Dick Hunt, was 'the weight-carrying hunter class of harness horse', which had to be immensely strong, as only two horses were employed to pull an omnibus which when fully loaded could weigh as much as three and a quarter tons. Most were mares, and were bought for about £35 each. The work was very hard, the more so because of all the stopping and starting, and the average working life of a bus horse was reckoned to be no more than five years, after which they fetched about £5. The working life expectancy of the horses which pulled the trams that appeared in later times was even lower – sometimes only two or two and a half years.

Some of the larger and more fashionable hotels, particularly in some of the resort towns, had their own private omnibuses which they used for collecting customers from the railway stations and for taking them out on excursions. They were small twelve-seater vehicles, as a rule, with the name of the establishment prominently displayed on the body panels. Others kept a small landaulette or 'fly' for this purpose.

Chapter 7
Trade vehicles

Carriages for private and public transport constituted only a limited percentage of the thousands of vehicles which could be seen on the streets of any market town or city during the eighteen hundreds, and the diversity and range of commercial vehicles showed that the builders of trade vehicles were every bit as skilled and inventive as their more prestigious carriage-building brethren. Everything from beer barrels to criminals, blocks of stone to dead horses, had to be transported by horse power, and a great many tradesmen depended on the horse for their livelihood. Ironically, although commercial vehicles were once so numerous, disappointingly few are in existence now. The reason is that private carriages were built to last, carefully maintained and used with discretion, and then when their working life was over many were left in coach houses and old barns to be discovered and restored to their former glory at later times. Commercial vehicles, on the other hand, were subjected to hard and often rough work until they either disintegrated or were sold for scrap, and those that were still in use when motorized transport came upon the scene were generally discarded, for no astute tradesmen could afford to waste valuable storage space on out-of-date equipment.

A smart turnout was a good advertisement for a tradesman, and some delivery vehicles in daily use could match the formal carriages of the wealthy for cleanliness and condition. All the fashionable city tailors, haberdashers and milliners provided a delivery service for their important customers, and for this they employed a delivery or omnibus van, which closely resembled a boxed-in brougham. These vehicles were beautifully painted, with the name of the firm written in ornate lettering on either side, and the driver and his assistant were dressed in smart livery to match the colour of the vehicle. In 1894 the Bristol Wagon and Carriage Works Co. advertised a version of this useful vehicle specially designed for bakers and confectioners, with:

> doors at back, body set low to the ground and convenient for loading, ventilators at sides, iron guard rails round roof for carrying parcels on top, best springs, patent axles and brass oil caps, lamps and brake complete, and either shafts for one horse or pole for a pair, as required. Painted and picked out in best style, and highly varnished.

The price was fifty-nine pounds complete. Less expensive models could also be supplied, including a neat two-wheeled delivery cart 'for bakers, confectioners, grocers, etc., requiring quick delivery to their customers', which cost only twenty-four pounds ten shillings. Not all tradesmen owned their own turnouts, however, and the ubiquitous jobmasters were always ready to provide any type of delivery vehicle, even one painted in the customer's own livery and displaying his name if the contract was regular and lucrative. A flashy or impressive horse or cob was essential and the London butchers and fishmongers were particularly renowned for their fast high-stepping cobs, many pure Hackney or Welsh Cob. In the days before refrigeration, a fast horse was very important for quick deliveries, because in hot weather the meat and fish soon went off. A similar vehicle was the game cart, which also had slatted sides for ventilation, but was further equipped with 'iron rods in the roof with hooks for carrying pheasants, grouse, etc.'. Fortnum and Masons' beautifully appointed delivery vehicles were a familiar sight in London streets during Victoria's reign.

A special favourite with the public was the dairyman's turnout, drawn by a strong sensible cob who soon learnt his job and would walk slowly from house to house, stopping while the milkman made the deliveries or waiting patiently at the dairy while the milk-float was loaded. The milk was carried in large brass churns and ladled out into the customers' jugs, and the milk-floats were specially designed to hold one or more churns, the driver having a folding seat near the front or, if space was especially short, a little occasional seat which could be hooked on to the side of the vehicle. Some floats were built in such a way that the driver could only get out by standing up and raising the hinged seat on which he had been sitting, and it is believed that the name 'trap' for small vehicles originated from carts of this design in which the driver was actually trapped while sitting down. The milk float was a two-wheeled cart with access from the rear. Floats varied from simple roughly constructed vehicles to more decorative examples like the 'Exhibition Float' designed and marketed by the Bristol Wagon and Carriage Works Co. and described in their catalogue as 'a very stylish cart, suitable for pony or cob, well adapted for wine merchants, grocers, aerated water trade or milk deliveries . . . good easy springs, portable seatboard, front nameboard and top nameboards each side, tailboard let down on chains. Very light in draught.' It retailed at twenty-one pounds, with the brass-mounted milk churns costing up to three pounds each, depending on the capacity. The same firm made another interesting type of milkfloat with 'an opening in the backboard for the tap of the milkcan to project through', this system replacing the old-fashioned ladle system which some considered unhygienic. When bottled milk came into vogue, specially constructed four-wheeled boxcarts with sliding side doors were introduced, and in 1890 an American milkman, John R. Parsons, patented his design for a four-wheeled delivery vehicle with the centre section of the body stepped for easy access. So successful were his 'Parsons' Low-down Wagons' that a factory was set up in Earlville, New York, to manufacture them. Rubber tyres and, later, pneumatic tyres were fitted to milk floats, as iron tyres were very noisy and disturbed people early in the mornings when the deliveries were being made.

Fresh fruit, vegetables and cut flowers were sold from two-wheeled flat carts or, in the early part of this century, four-wheeled trolleys with a cover which protected the merchandise from the ravages of the weather. Many grocers used a market cart for their trade, as this two-wheeled covered van was light but roomy enough to carry a large stock of goods. The driver's seat was little more than a flat board reached by means of a step and an iron tread plate on the shaft. Under the canvas hood, held up by bentwood hoops, were arranged the shelves, including a flat plank for the weights and scales which all British tradesmen were obliged by law to carry. Some of the larger grocers also kept one or more covered vans or wagons for the collection of bulk consignments from markets, mills and railway stations. Laundry vans were always four-wheeled, with high, wood-panelled bodies and double doors at the rear, although some were also built with access from behind the driver's seat. The interior provided plenty of room for the enormous wicker laundry baskets, stacked one on top of another. Most tradesmen's vehicles were drawn by one horse only, the laundry firms favouring a stronger vanner type, but the delivery broughams of the fashionable milliners and gown shops were sometimes drawn by a matched pair, as it looked impressive when making a delivery at a private house.

Towards the second half of the nineteenth century ice-cream vendors, many of them Italian immigrants, began appearing on the streets of most of the main European cities and their gaily coloured two-wheeled carts became a welcome sight on hot days. They were drawn by quiet ponies which were led rather than driven, as there was no driver's seat, and the square-panelled body with glass windows was entered through a door at the back. Red-and-white-striped awnings supported by twisted brass rods shaded the brass-lidded containers which were kept submerged in a bed of ice at the front of the vehicle. There were several ice merchants in London who supplied the ice-cream makers with their essential commodity, and their light fast carts were to be seen dashing from the docks, where they bought the ice straight off Scandinavian ships, to the premises of their Italian customers.

For anyone moving house, the services of a furniture remover had to be called upon, and their enormous vans drawn by a pair of very heavy draught horses were capable of holding an immense amount of furniture and household goods. There was even room on the roof for smaller items, which could be covered with a tarpaulin. The floor of the rear half of the van was built in the form of a well to provide more space, and the high tailboard let down to form a ramp up which the furniture could be carried. The driver occupied a small seat at the front of the roof, and the whole vehicle was garishly painted with the firm's name and the extent of their services in large colourful letters.

Some of the most impressive horses were the heavy horses used by the breweries, many of which still employ horses to this day for deliveries in the vicinity of the brewery yard, as well as for publicity purposes. The first brewery drays were the long two-wheeled carts originally used in Georgian times and capable of carrying up to five barrels, each holding one hundred and eight gallons. They were pulled by two strong horses harnessed one in front of the other, and supervised by a foot drover armed with a whip and not unlike the stage-wagon drivers of the previous century. Four-wheeled drays were introduced when smaller casks came to be used and these were drawn by a pair of horses or, if the load was abnormally heavy, a 'unicorn' of two horses at the back and one at the front. The panelled or railed sides often let down to facilitate loading and unloading, and the driver had a high seat at the front. Quite often the drivers got drunk while on their rounds and the patient and intelligent horses had to find their own way home while their attendants slept on the back of the dray.

The coalmen used a similar type of horse to that of the breweries for drawing their four-wheeled coal carts, which when loaded could weigh as much as three tons. Coal carts were built to a number of different designs, ranging from the beautiful bow-fronted, spindle-sided London type with a let-down tailboard and an ornate nameboard at the front from behind which the vehicle was driven, to the plainer lumber wagons of American design. By 1893 Londoners alone burned something like eight million tons of coal a year, so the coal business was a busy and profitable one. Most coal horses did not start work until they were five-year-olds and were gradually introduced to the work until eventually they did a six-day week, being rested on a Sunday. They worked long hours but were compensated with frequent lengthy breaks while the wagons were loaded at the depot or unloaded at the customer's premises. Even so, coal horses rarely lasted in the job for longer than nine or ten years, some not even as long as that, after which they went like so many others to the repository where they might fetch about ten pounds. Some of these worn-out horses were bought by bathing machine proprietors, who used them for hauling in and out of the water the ungainly wheeled huts in which Victorian bathers protected their modesty. The work was not hard and the sea water was excellent for the legs, and many horses returned to the streets again after a season or two at the seaside.

In Britain, the Post Office operated a service of horse-drawn mail vans for carrying the mail bags to the various starting points where the mail coaches picked them up. Even in much later times, these handy two-wheeled vehicles were still in use for relaying the mail between the sorting offices and railway stations or for delivering it in remote country districts. Although all the vehicles had to be painted scarlet, with the words 'Royal Mail' together with the royal cypher on the side panels so that they were immediately recognizable, the actual vehicles were not all built to the same design. This was because only a limited number of the large four-wheeled vans used in the towns were actually owned by the Post Office; the rest were hired on contract from individuals who often worked for the Post Office. One such person was George Tyson, the Coniston postman, who in 1910 was under contract to supply his own horse and cart for delivering the letters around his home area. Like many others with a similar job, he used a vehicle that was not unlike a two-wheeled butcher's cart with a boxed-in body to keep the letters dry in bad weather. The mail, including parcels, was delivered in the Grasmere area by means of a smart four-wheeled delivery van which was owned by the Post Office, although a local coach firm, Riggs of Windermere, having successfully tendered for the Windermere to Keswick mail contract, supplied the horses and driver. Another firm contracting for the Post Office was McNamara's, who from the 1880s provided most of the parcel mail vans that left London for such destinations as Oxford. Many of these mail vans ran through the night in order to make delivery deadlines, and as late as 1909 there were still at least six of these vehicles running regularly out of the capital.

The building trade made use of horse-drawn vehicles for transporting their materials to the sites where they were working, and in Britain most conformed to a standard design, with a deep square body complete with removable tailboard and straight shafts. Most had two wheels only, and a number had solid shelving which projected over the front and sides so that an extra load could be carried. Another type of vehicle this busy trade employed was the stone or marble cart, a heavily built two-wheeled cart which resembled a Roman chariot in outline, with its high rounded front and open back. Like the builder's cart, it was drawn by one horse, unless the hills it had to climb were so steep that a 'chain' or 'cock' horse had to be harnessed in front to help it up. Chain horses were kept at the bottom of hills solely for this job and it cost one penny to recruit their assistance. Some dishonest and unscrupulous drivers were content to let their horses struggle to the top of the hill unaided, although they did not forget to charge their employer the penny for the chain horse when they got back, as it made a welcome supplement to a meagre wage. The drivers of the long timber carts carrying tree trunks also used this trick to their pecuniary advantage.

The most sinister of all commercial vehicles was the four-wheeled enclosed van used for transporting prisoners between police station, court room and prison. The black-painted vehicles had small barred windows on each side and a platform at the back with grab handles where one of the escorting officers could ride. The name 'Black Maria' by which these grim vehicles came to be known owed its origins to an American Negress called Maria Lee who was famous for her dealings with trouble-makers in her home town of Boston, Massachusetts. The vans were drawn by a pair of sombre-coloured horses and driven by a policeman from the raised boxseat at the front.

The first fire engines were owned by large private estates and maintained for their own use only. They were small hand-pumped vehicles usually filled from a nearby lake or river. In cities, some insurance companies owned their own fire engines and operated them for their own benefit when the premises of their customers caught fire. By Victorian times the pair-horse fire engine was a magnificent machine, with steam boilers capable of pumping out up to three hundred and fifty gallons of water a minute. The horses were stabled in pairs with the harness hung directly above them to facilitate a quick 'put to' in the event of the fire brigade being summoned. The sight of the fire engine dashing through the streets, with the horses galloping, the bell ringing, and the boiler belching sparks, was something all children loved to see. Ambulance horses were also stabled in pairs ready for an emergency, and the ambulance itself was often a converted brougham or covered four-wheeled van.

For the funeral trade, a special breed of black horse from Holland and Belgium was favoured. They were preferred to other breeds because of their size, stately bearing and superb depth of colour, without any tendency to dark brown. These Flemish horses were known as the 'Black Brigade'; they were imported into England and America as three-year-olds and took about a year to train before they were actually used in a funeral cortège. The hearses were oblong, glass-sided and mounted on four wheels, with a boxseat at the front which was usually covered with a fringed black or purple hammercloth, although some were carved wood made to look like folded cloth and painted. Access was through double glass doors at the back of the vehicle and the roof was decorated at the corners with black ostrich plumes. The harness was black and encrusted with silver fittings, and the long black velvet loin cloths worn by the pair of horses which drew the hearse reached almost to the ground. Black ostrich plumes were fitted to the crown-pieces of the bridles, too. At large or important funerals four horses were occasionally used to pull the hearse, and the deceased's family and friends followed behind in black-plumed mourning coaches, many of them black-painted broughams driven by employees of the funeral director. In 1790 there was only one funeral director or 'black master' in London, but a hundred years later there were several dozen of them, employing over seven hundred Flemish horses for nothing else but funeral work. At such times as influenza epidemics when the death rate rose unexpectedly and the black masters were hard pressed to cope, they sometimes had to hire brown or bay horses from the jobmasters in order to relieve their own overworked animals. The largest firm in London was Dottridges, who not only prided themselves on having buried some of the most famous people in the city, but also supplied all the requisites for the trade to most of the other funeral directors too.

One of the most common trade vehicles to be seen was the carrier cart, which could be two- or four-wheeled, open or closed, depending on what was to be carried in it. Carriers were literally haulage contractors and many of them had long-term contracts with particular firms or organizations, while others were prepared to do anything that would bring in a few pounds. The railways used carts for delivering all types of freight, from perishable products destined for shops and stores to live animals, and although some of the vehicles were on contract, others belonged to them. The railways also used horses on the lines to shunt the railway carriages and trucks which contained all sorts of cargo including cattle. Apart from being extremely strong, for the trucks were immensely heavy and difficult to get started, the shunting horses had to be well trained so that they could be controlled by word of mouth. A similar sort of job was performed by the barge horses which were once a familiar sight on the towpaths that run alongside the canals of England. They were usually led, or occasionally ridden, and they pulled the barge by a long rope that was attached at one end to the swingletree connected to the horse's traces and at the other to the bows of the barge. The barges carried loads of up to fifty tons and it took both strength and skill to keep the barge moving without being dragged backwards into the canal.

Most country towns had never seen a horse-drawn bulk tanker or even an omnibus until quite late in the nineteenth century, while farmers' spring carts laden with produce were something of a rarity in inner-city districts. The municipal vestry horse and his heavy four-wheeled dustcart were to be encountered almost everywhere where there was horse traffic, for the amount of dung on the roads was always a serious problem. In the 1890s it was estimated that thirteen hundred thousand cartloads of refuse, much of it manure, were carried out of London alone each year, and an incredible fifteen hundred horses were employed for this operation. The name 'vestry' came into use because the local authorities who were responsible for controlling the job of removing refuse from the roads had regular meetings which were originally held in the vestry of a church or in a parish hall. In small towns and country areas, a lighter two-wheeled tumbler cart which could be drawn by a cob was preferred to a big dustcart. The body of the tumbler cart was made from iron plates which were welded together to form a drum-shaped watertight container with a lid at the top, and the whole body tipped for emptying. After wet weather, tumbler carts were used to cart away the mud that workmen had laboriously shovelled out of drainage channels or from kerbsides. Another municipal vehicle was the two-wheeled road scraper, which resembled an enormous comb and was employed for collecting dung into heaps before the dustcart came along. After rainstorms the vestry horse could have as much as three tons to pull, although in fine weather the absence of water could reduce the load by several hundredweight. Sir John Whitworth, an eminent engineer, invented a horse-drawn mechnical roadsweeper which was first tried out in Manchester in 1844, but it was regarded as a gimmick and never caught on.

With so many horses on the roads and no proper system of traffic contol, the number of accidents was, not surprisingly, high, and fallen or injured horses were a common sight in the busy city streets. In 1863, up to twenty thousand vehicles crossed London Bridge every day between eight in the

Figure 8 Tipping tumbler cart used for the removal of horse manure from the streets.

morning and eight in the evening. Two-wheeled knackers' carts fitted with a winch to haul the dead horse into the vehicle were always in demand, and occasionally high-sided horse ambulances with a ramp at the back for access into the low-slung body could be seen, although they were more common at racecourses. The military authorities of a number of countries also employed horse ambulances in the days when cavalry regiments were used in warfare. Horse-drawn horseboxes were very rare and only used for expensive racehorses which were considered too valuable to be led or ridden from place to place (the usual practice).

No city was complete without its costermongers with their brightly painted barrows laden with fruit, vegetables, flowers or firewood, and drawn by a smart pony, or if they were less affluent, a donkey. Some costermongers were more like general dealers, and used a large four-wheeled enclosed wagon to display their wares, which might range from rugs and brushes to chairs, hardware and ornaments. Known affectionately as 'cheap-jacks', these nomadic traders wandered from town to town during the summer months selling their wares where they could find customers. Another nomad was the travelling showman with his mobile cage on wheels, drawn by a quiet horse of the vanner type which was often piebald or skewbald in order to be as conspicuous as possible, and containing performing dogs, monkeys, exotic birds, fighting cocks and 'rare animals from the depths of darkest Africa'. His horse-drawn cage was his advertisement, and a travelling showman always received a warm welcome when he arrived in a village, where, with the help of his animals, a few enthralling stories and a conjuring trick or two, he could put on a performance for the local people. Travelling circuses and menageries were also very popular, and they used a variety of two- and four-wheeled carts and wagons to carry all their equipment, roundabouts, mechanical organs and animals. Enormous oblong barred cages with folding shutters, mounted on four small wheels, were used as a travelling home for lions, tigers and wolves, these being particular favourites with the public. The firm of Savage and Co., of Kings Lynn in Norfolk, specialized in showman's vehicles and some of their living vans, especially the so-called saloon type, were masterpieces of design and craftsmanship. By 1890, there were over twelve thousand gipsies in England alone and many more in the other European countries, and their colourful horse-drawn caravans or vardies were built to a number of patterns, including bow-top, burton and ledge. Many were very ornate, with beautifully carved undercarriages and fine paintwork including much gold leaf. Dark colours like crimson were favoured, but never yellow, as the superstitious gipsies considered this a 'poverty' colour. The interiors were even more lavish, with clerestory roofs, engraved or frosted glass windows, fitted fine wood furnishings including many mirrors which gave an illusion of extra space, a queenie stove, and specially constructed racks to display the superb china so beloved of travelling people.

Other commercial vehicles which catered for specialist trades were sometimes seen, like the long narrow carts used by chimney sweeps for carrying their brushes, the bulk tankers which appeared towards the turn of the century for transporting paraffin or chemicals, and the colossally heavy carts drawn by teams of six horses and used by local authority workers for breaking up the surfaces of roads requiring rebuilding. Large numbers of ponies were employed in the mining industry for hauling the coal tubs along the tracks either above ground or actually down the mines themselves.

Farm vehicles changed surprisingly little over the years. Most were the work of local village craftsmen rather than large-scale builders, and to this can be attributed the national and regional variations in farm wagons. Many of the designs can be traced back to the carriers' stage wagons, which they resembled except that the canvas hood had been discarded, but those vehicles for use on heavy clay ground were built with very broad wheels, while those for light sandy areas like the farmland of Eastern Europe were built with lighter frames and narrower wheels. The wain, a two-wheeled flat platform with boarded protectors over the wheels and railed extensions at the front and back to hold the load in place, was much used in the sixteenth and seventeenth centuries, and the two-wheeled dung cart, which could also be employed for carting root crops and building materials, developed from it, as it was found to be easier to turn on wet or muddy ground than a four-wheeled wagon. An ingenious vehicle of English design was the hermaphrodite wagon which appeared in the early nineteenth century. This was really a two-wheeled cart to which could be attached an extra pair of wheels in the form of a forecarriage for supporting a horizontal platform, thereby greatly increasing the carrying capacity. Hermaphrodite wagons cost about twenty pounds, which was less than half the price of a four-wheeled wagon, and as the forecarriage could be easily detached after harvest time, the rear part of the vehicle could be used as an ordinary farm cart for the rest of the year. In addition to the farm wagons and carts, there was a whole range of horse-drawn implements, including reapers, seed drills, ploughs and harrows. In forest areas a useful vehicle was the timber bob, which consisted of a pair of wheels mounted on a bowed axle from which the log was suspended by chains, though for very large pieces of timber a four-wheeled version was sometimes used.

As with all horse-drawn vehicles, individual requirements gave rise to one-off vehicles specially built to the precise orders of discerning customers, a service that was virtually lost when mass production methods put many small vehicle-building firms out of business.

Chapter 8

Dangerous travel

Despite the unremitting attempts of engineers, coach builders and inventors, no absolutely safe method of road travel was ever devised, although the situation was certainly not as bad as one early nineteenth-century traveller suggested it might be when he advised other travellers to make out their wills before embarking on a journey. Runaway horses, broken vehicles, drunken coachmen, bad weather, highwaymen and a dozen other dangers often made for adventurous journeys, not to count the severe discomforts caused by the deficiencies of carriage suspension and the dreadful condition of the roads.

The early stage wagons travelled so slowly that the only real danger associated with them was that they were liable to disintegrate as they lurched and rocked over the uneven road surfaces that were mountainous enough in places actually to throw them over. The stage and mail coaches that superseded them had better roads to travel on, but their design and the fact that they travelled at speeds of up to ten miles an hour, which was considered excessively fast, made them susceptible to turning over too, often with disastrous results. During the Regency period a number of so-called safety coaches built with low centres of gravity or various types of skid intended to keep the coach upright in the event of a wheel coming off appeared on the road, and in 1819 a patent safety coach called the 'Sovereign' went into service on the London-to-Brighton road. By 1830 there were dozens of safety coaches in use, but few offered any real advantages over those they were supposedly replacing, except that no passengers or luggage were carried on the roof, thereby helping to minimize the top-heaviness that had been typical of earlier coaches. In 1795, John Hatchett of London designed a most ingenious coach for the Marquis of Lansdown, which had the body mounted between two swivels so that it always remained upright even if the vehicle turned right over, and other coach-building firms patented assorted safety devices which, according to their catalogues, made their vehicles safe conveyances 'for the most timid persons'. Owners of private carriages were equally at risk and Sir George Stephen remarked in *The Groom* how he had 'received a concussion of the brain from the neglect of my servant in passing over a broken shaft in my Stanhope (gig) which he daily cleaned'.

No vehicle was ever immune from the depredations of highwaymen and outlaws, most of whom were brutal degenerate men for whom hard work was an abomination. Others saw robbery as a short cut to wealth, and a newspaper of 1774 reported that seven highwaymen recently imprisoned had proved to be the sons of well-to-do families. Few English roads were free from highwaymen during their heyday between 1650 and 1750, but by the days of the mail coaches with their armed guards highwaymen had virtually died out – although between 1806 and 1824 six highwaymen were hanged at Fisherton goal. Pepys recorded in his diary that on 11 April 1661, 'Mrs Anne and I rode under a man that hangs upon Shooters Hill, and a filthy sight it was to see how his flesh is shrunk to the bones.' Horace Walpole, writing in 1781, expressed the opinion that 'unless country squires would take time off from shooting partridges and shoot highwaymen instead society would be dissolved'. (See R.C. and S.M. Anderson, *Quicksilver*, 1973.)

The most famous but the most overrated highwayman was Dick Turpin, who was born in 1705 in Essex and who, at one time, had his own business as a butcher in Whitechapel. He avoided the tiresome formality of buying and paying for his cattle by stealing them on a large scale, and from such dishonest beginnings he went on to become one of the most celebrated highwaymen of his time. He was hanged in 1739. Another infamous highwayman was Claude du Vall, who stopped a coach carrying a wealthy gentleman and his beautiful wife and proceeded to ask the lady if she would dance with him. This she consented to, while her terrified husband provided music by singing and playing a flageolet. After the dance du Vall handed the lady back into the coach and robbed her husband of four hundred pounds. Another highwayman, Ned Wicks, once stopped Lord Mohun's private coach with the usual words, 'Stand and deliver', and was surprised and amused to be sworn at in the vilest language by Lord Mohun. Wicks decided that they should have a swearing match for a bet of thirty pounds with the coachman acting as judge, and for a full quarter of an hour the two men hurled invective at each other to the astonishment of the coachman, who prudently declared Wicks the winner, even though his employer swore 'as well as ever I heard any gentleman of quality in my life'. Even Oxford undergraduates were not above supplementing their meagre incomes with a little highway robbery, and Dr Routh, president of Magdalen College, admitted seeing 'two undergraduates hanged on Gownsmans Gallows in Holywell – hanged, sir, for highway robbery!' (V.A. Wilson, *The Coaching Era*.)

Although the Post Office took great pains to ensure that its coaches were regularly serviced and checked for defective parts, this was not always the case with other road users, including stage-coach proprietors, and a great many accidents were caused by parts of the harness or vehicle being weak or damaged. The Rockingham coach once lost a front wheel so unexpectedly that both the coachman and guard were thrown to the road, while the horses bolted. The front axle of the Worcestershire Telegraph once broke at the bottom of Hanwell Hill, causing the coach to crash over on its side, seriously injuring the coachman and passengers, including two ladies of whom 'little hope was entertained for their recovery'. Broken harness was responsible for many accidents, and the Bentham Mail narrowly avoided a serious crash when one of the horses shied and the coach hit the low parapet of a bridge. The reins broke, and the horse dashed off at full gallop with the laden coach rolling from side to side and in imminent danger of overturning. A toll-gate keeper, seeing them coming, had the presence of mind to shut the gate, and the coach ground to a halt with no serious injuries sustained by the passengers. Less fortunate were the passengers of the Bath coach which upset at Marlborough, resulting in a broken leg apiece for the coachman and a lady passenger, who were placed side by side in a wheelbarrow by willing helpers and trundled off to the nearest doctor.

Travellers on the North American stage coaches had to contend not only with outlaws, but also war parties of Red Indians, who would immobilize the coach by shooting one of the wheel horses, then set about the luckless passengers. Travellers on coaches in Argentina had to put up with 'merciless Indians, struggling through bogs, crossing streams, depending on horses never well fed, always over-worked and sometimes wretchedly thin . . . drought or deluge, intense heat or bitterest cold, dust, flies, mosquitoes, lack of drinking water'. (C. Jewell, *Argentina Stage Coaches*, 1966.)

Incompetent driving not infrequently resulted in accidents, although in England any coachman found liable through negligence could expect a heavy fine and immediate dismissal with little hope of being employed elsewhere. In 1839 the Newcastle-bound Mail veered off the road, then plunged into a quarry when the coachman obstinately refused to slow down despite the fog which was so dense he could not see his leaders from the boxseat. Jack Creery, coachman of the Lancaster and Kirkby Stephen Mail, was once so drunk that he had to hand over the reins to the guard, who was so intoxicated himself that they got lost, and it was not just the elements which gave one Northumbrian coachman his red nose; it was the twenty brandies he drank every day before he climbed on to the coach. A collision between two coaches near Biggleswade in 1837 was put down to the fact that one of the coachmen was so drunk that he did not see the other approaching. The drunken offender was hurled from the coach and killed outright, along with two of the unfortunate horses.

When the craze for learning to drive swept the young gentry, a new hazard presented itself for passengers. Many coachmen were prepared for a small fee to let the aspiring driver take the reins for part of the journey, much to the consternation of the other passengers, although most professional coachmen took their work as instructors seriously and were strict masters. A disgruntled pupil of Bill Williams, driver of the Oxford Defiance, complained in an article in the *New Sporting Magazine* that his tutor would never 'allow an error or an ungraceful act pass un-noticed, and I have often got off his box so annoyed at his merciless reproofs and lectures that I vowed no power on earth should make me touch another rein for him'. One young blood, having bribed the coachman of the Cambridge Star to let him drive, allowed the horses to go too fast with the result that the coach tipped over and one of the passengers, Mr Calloway, the champion jockey who was on his way to Newmarket Races, broke a leg. He sued the coach proprietors and was awarded £2,000 in compensation.

Racing between rival coaches, though illegal, was another practice which alarmed passengers because it encouraged coachmen to take unreasonable risks at their expense. The drivers of the fast stage coaches were often tempted to try and outpace the mails, and despite the heavy fines imposed on offenders, some proprietors even encouraged racing as it appealed to their sporting instincts. In practice, more bones were broken than records, and some horrible accidents ensued. A report in the *Leeds Mercury* in 1826, referring to 'another of those accidents to which stage coach passengers are so much exposed' told how

> both the coaches from Leeds to York entered the town at full gallop and the True Briton, in attempting to pass the other coach, ran over a basket of dung which stood in its way, and was overturned. At the time when the incident happened, the coach had six inside and four outside passengers; but though the position of all the passengers was perilous in the extreme, only one lady passenger received any material hurt. The lady, who was one of the inside passengers, finding that the coach was likely to upset, seized hold of the door, and the coach falling upon her hand, either crushed off all her fingers, or bruised them so terribly, so as to render amputation necessary.

The Holyhead and Chester mail coaches collided near St Albans in 1820 while racing, and the two coachmen were sentenced to twelve months each in jail as a result of one of the passengers being killed. Another contest between two Greenwich coaches in 1815 frightened the passengers so much that several threw themselves from the coach in sheer despair, including one gentleman who 'fell on his face against the gravel with such force that his nose was flattened'.

Some accidents were the fault of interfering bystanders, like the boy who without thinking cracked the whip which the coachman had left on the boxseat while he went into an inn at Ewell in 1826. The startled horses bolted down the street and crashed into a fence, throwing off all the outside passengers, including a lady who, according to the local newspaper, died 'in the greatest agony'. Her gravestone in Ewell churchyard reads: 'Catherine, wife of James Bailey, who in consequence of the overturning of the Dorking coach April 1826 met with her death in the twenty second year of her age.' Other mishaps were often blamed on other careless road users, like the collision between the Coburg coach and a wagon in 1918 which killed the coachman and two passengers.

Some of the collisions and overturns were genuine accidents for which no one could be fairly blamed, like the incident in 1838 when one of the leaders of the Edinburgh to Perth coach, which was being loaded at Newhall's Quay, South Queensferry, shied and the coach-and-four plunged over the quay wall, causing two inside passengers to drown. Ten years earlier, the Alnwick to Newcastle coach had been crossing Morpeth bridge when the horses shied at some carts and rocked the coach so violently that three passengers were tossed into the swirling Wansbeck river below. Floods and weak or damaged bridges were sometimes the cause of the whole equipage being swept away, as happened to the Liverpool Mail in September 1829 which suffered the deaths of three passengers and all four horses. One of the most treacherous coach routes anywhere was the ten-mile strip of land across Morecambe Bay from Hest Bank to Ulverston, which was passable only at low tide, and even then there were dangerous gullies and areas of quicksand. The coaches were guided by mounted guides with long poles which they used to search out patches of shifting sand into which the coach could sink, and after dusk a powerful light was lit in an upper room of the Hest Bank Hotel to act as a beacon for the coachmen. Even so, in 1828 a coach caught fast in the sands and the passengers were lucky to escape, while twenty-two years later a coach disappeared completely while crossing the sands and no trace of it was ever seen again.

Not all mishaps ended in disaster, however, and there was an amusing story concerning an elderly gentleman who was the only inside passenger on a coach travelling from Carlisle to Newcastle in 1839. The coach bounced over a heap of gravel at the side of the road, throwing off both the driver and the guard, who had clambered across the roof to try to stop the bolting horses, and the horses galloped on for another seven miles. When they stopped, the solitary passenger who got out to remonstrate with the coachman for going too fast was devastated to find there was no one there but himself. Another favourite anecdote of old coachmen concerned Mrs Cox, an 'immense woman' who kept a fish stall in Devonport Market, and who was being handed a glass of wine by the waiter at an inn at Yealmpton when the horses, left unattended and hearing a movement on the roof where Mrs Cox was sitting, presumed it was the coachman and set off at their usual pace. Mrs Cox was frightened to scream in case it startled the horses, and her frantic arm waving was to no avail, so she was obliged to keep her seat while the horses trotted the seven miles to Plymouth, where it took 'a considerable amount of gin' to soothe her nerves. What is perhaps most incredible about the story is that the horses, knowing the road well, managed to avoid other road traffic as well as crossing a bridge and passing through a toll bar without any problem.

Winter travel was always particularly hazardous, and the sporting-print image of the mail coach half submerged in a deep snowdrift, while the guard rode one of the horses over the horizon carrying the mailbags on his back, was often a reality. On 24 February 1838, the Edinburgh Mail, heading south, became marooned in a twelve-foot snow drift about seven miles north of Alnwick and the passengers had to struggle across the fields to North Charlton where they stayed for four days. Two years earlier, at Christmastide 1836, England had been subjected to the heaviest snow-storms within living memory of most people, and a writer in *The Times* commented that never before was the London Mail 'stopped for a whole night at a few miles from London'. Another writer of the day remarked that on 27 December no less than fourteen mail coaches had to be abandoned, although 'in all cases the bags were removed, the horses extricated'. So notable were the efforts by the guards to get the mail delivered that the Post Office Superintendent of the Mails issued the following acknowledgement to all mail guards: 'I have hourly proofs of the great exertions made by the guards to get the mails forwarded through the snow, and almost wonders have been performed, this is most gratifying to the Post Master General.' One mail guard who abandoned the coach for one of the horses and proceeded on foot when the drifts became too deep for even the horse, was found frozen to death in the snow with the mailbags still around his neck.

Perhaps the most bizarre 'accident' ever recorded in coaching annals occurred one October night in 1816 when the Exeter Mail was crossing Salisbury Plain and the coachman noticed a large animal, which he thought was a calf, creep out of the shadows and trot alongside the horses, which became very restless. When they drew up at Winterslow Hut to deliver the mailbags, the animal revealed itself to be a fully grown lioness which immediately sprang upon the off-leader. In the furore, two men rushed up with a mastiff dog which began baiting the lioness until she retreated to the cover of a nearby building, where she was later recaptured by the men who apparently owned the travelling menagerie from which she had escaped. Although the horse was dreadfully mauled, the men bought it and nursed it back to health, after which they exhibited it along with the lioness and the mastiff in their menagerie, admission costing 'one shilling for ladies and gentlemen, and sixpence for children and others'. The Louth Mail was once overturned in a ditch when the horses took fright at a donkey rolling in the dusty road, a humiliating experience for the proud coachman.

Travellers were even at risk from fire, and on one occasion in 1814 the Dover coach was 'delayed two hours by the wheel catching fire', this presumably being the result of an overheating axle. It is recorded that sparks from axle friction were the cause of a wagon in Northamptonshire catching fire in 1776. Unfortunately, the wagon was loaded with gunpowder, which exploded killing the wagon driver, the passengers and the horses. A similar incident occurred in Staffordshire a few years later, when the explosion 'shook the whole village and scattered the limbs of the horses and driver to a great distance'.

Coach travellers had to be ready to expect almost anything when it came to travelling companions, and one gentleman boarded a night coach to discover next morning that the fur-coated gentleman he had been chatting to overnight had been a performing bear. Another gentleman found himself sharing the cramped coach with two lunatics on their way to an asylum, while two ladies boarding a coach at Chelmsford found that the only seats left were inside, where there was already one other lady who had died about an hour earlier. Rather than walk, the two women climbed in and sat uncomfortably watching the corpse for the rest of their journey. One infamous Newcastle-upon-Tyne coachman with an unpleasant sense of humour used to slap one of the trunks on the roof of the coach and terrify the passengers by shouting to the guard, 'What sort of choice corpse have you picked out this time for your medical friends?' Suspicions of a busy traffic in human bodies between grave robbers and the Edinburgh lecturers in anatomy led to some investigations into the matter. In September 1825, a coach trunk with a 'putrid smell' was opened by the authorities and found to contain the body of a young woman; two other bodies were later discovered at the Turks Head Hotel in Newcastle awaiting transportation to Edinburgh. Dangerous criminals were also carried on coaches, to the terror of the other passengers. Dickens described in *Great Expectations* how convicts usually sat on the roof with their ironed legs dangling over the edges, and in 1779 Charles Wesley travelled in a coach with ten convicts in the basket at the back and was deeply shocked at the way in which they were 'loudly blaspheming'.

Travelling in towns and cities was considerably more dangerous than it is today because of the great volume of traffic and the fact that road users were subject to few rules and regulations. Although most Londoners were aware by 1868, when traffic signals were first introduced into the capital, that they should keep to the left-hand side of the road, many refused to do so despite the efforts of the police. Cab and omnibus drivers thought nothing of darting across the road in the face of oncoming traffic to pick up a fare, and costermongers only increased the congestion by parking their barrows anywhere they felt might be good for trade. Commercial vehicles were dangerously overloaded, especially timber and carriers' carts, which were sometimes loaded up to a height of twelve or even fifteen feet. Carters tended to feel that because of the enormous size of their vehicles they had the right of way, and *Punch* magazine continually satirized them in cartoons showing smaller vehicles scurrying out of the way of the carter's wagons. One of the reasons why large vehicles so often monopolized the crown of the road was that the cambered sides were frequently worn slippery, and shopkeepers objected to having grit or sand put down to give a better grip for the horses because the particles blew on to their outside displays. Comparing the value of the three types of road surface in use in London, William Heywood, a surveyor, found that on average a horse could only travel 191 miles on asphalt, 132 on granite sets, and 330 on wooden blocks before it fell. In bad weather, the streets were littered with fallen horses and in the severe snowstorms of 1886 it is recorded that forty-nine horses died and another thousand were injured. Fog was often to blame for collisions, which in many cases proved fatal for the horses, and many people had special strengthened boards built into the back of their carriages to protect them from the pole of a colliding vehicle bursting through the rear panel. In the packed streets many horses were run through by the shafts of other vehicles, and runaways were quite frequent. Policemen were instructed to patrol the kerbside at their regulation two and a half miles an hour ready to leap out and stop bolting horses if the occasion arose, and wise pedestrians were always prepared to jump into doorways at a moment's notice should the cry of 'runaway' be heard. Even Queen Victoria was involved in a number of accidents, including one in the Highlands in 1863 when her carriage turned right over and she was lucky to escape with little more than bruises and shock.

When the railways began to threaten the supremacy of horse-drawn transport, the cab and coach proprietors were quick to point out some of the dangers inherent in the new system. They frightened their passengers off the railways as best they could with horrific stories of derailments and exploding boilers, and are said to have asked them, 'When a coach upsets there you are, but when a train upsets where are you?' When James Huskinson was run over and killed at the opening of the Liverpool and Manchester Railway, the coachmen said it was an omen of things to come, but most knew deep down that the days of horse-drawn transport were numbered.

Chapter 9
In decline

In 1791, Dr Erasmus Darwin published a remarkable prophecy in which he foretold the demise of horse-drawn transport in favour of railways, motor-cars and even aeroplanes:

> Soon shall thy arm unconquered steam afar,
> Drag the slow barge, or drive the rapid car;
> Or on wide waving wings expanded bear,
> The flying chariot through the fields of air.

William Murdoch, emulating the example of the French engineer Nicholas Joseph Cugnot who built his first steam engine in 1769, was probably the first Englishman seriously to consider steam as a means of power. He produced a steam-driven vehicle in 1784 that was capable of pulling a small wagon around his home in Redruth, Cornwall, and he was responsible for interesting other inventors in this system of transport. By 1838, there were seven important steam-carriage companies in existence and they operated a number of services out of London, Liverpool and several other major cities. At first, people regarded them with hostility; they were dirty, noisy, they frightened horses and they were considered a source of potential danger. Some people even tried to get them banned on the grounds that they were a 'public nuisance', but their complaints were futile, although in some areas the steam carriages were attacked by members of the public who hurled stones at the hissing monstrosities. The toll road proprietors did not like them either, as they tended to churn up the road surfaces, and the turnpikes accordingly charged them an inflated toll fee or banned them altogether. It is recorded that a coach-and-four could travel from Liverpool to Prescot and pay only four shillings in tolls, whereas a steam carriage would have to pay two pounds eight shillings to do exactly the same journey. These and other problems, including the cost of purchasing and running steam carriages, made them economically unsuccessful and they soon disappeared from the roads.

For many years the mines had been using small horse drawn trucks on rails for carrying coal, and the idea of a similar system for transporting freight between towns seemed a logical progression. The use of steam power instead of horses soon followed, and the railways were born, with the first line laid between Stockton and Darlington in 1825. In an age of rapid technological advancement the railways spread, according to one old coach guard, 'like a plague', and left the coach-and-four a slow and outdated means of transport. 'In 1835,' wrote Stanley Harris in *The Coaching Age*, (1885) 'there was not a railway out of London,' yet in less than a few decades nearly every town and village in the country was covered by the vast network of railways. *The Times* expressed the opinion in 1839 that 'steam, James Watt and George Stephenson have a great deal to answer for. They will ruin the breed of horses, as they have already ruined the innkeepers and coachmen, many of whom have already been obliged to seek relief at the poorhouse, or have died in penury and want.'

In spite of the bitter rivalry between the railway companies and the coachmen, there were attempts at liaison for the benefit of both parties and on 22 May 1838 the Post Office announced a new departure:

The Mails to Holyhead, Manchester, Liverpool and Carlisle are to be despatched tonight for the first time by the London and Birmingham railway. The coaches are to be drawn by horses to the terminus at Euston Square, and there to be placed on trucks and so run on the railway, retaining their coachmen, guards, passengers, etc., and only requiring horses when they reach the end of the railway to proceed on to their respective journeys.

The London to Louth mailcoach left Louth on its last journey on 19 December 1845 on the back of a railway wagon on the newly opened Peterborough to Blisworth line. Some coach proprietors with the foresight to realize that steam had come to stay sold out lock, stock and barrel, one of these being William Chaplin who astutely sold his thirteen hundred horses and went on to invest in the railway companies, but some, like Sherman, with a stable of seven hundred horses, hung on doggedly and lost huge amounts of money by their action. When Birch Reynardson, a wealthy amateur, wanted to sell his coach which had cost one hundred and thirteen pounds to have built, Tattersalls could only get six pounds for it. The famous long-distance coaches were the first to come off the road, followed by the provincial coaches, a few of which continued to run in isolated areas long after the expansion of the railways. Most coaches were left in stableyards until they rotted away or were sold for scrap, and several were bought for a few pounds by farmers who transferred the wheels to other vehicles and used the bodies for hen huts. The Venture was used as a hen house on a Yorkshire farm for years before it was discovered and renovated, while the Yorkshire Hero was found rotting in a corner of a field. The harness usually sold quite well, as it could be used in other spheres of horse-drawn transport, and the same generally applied to the horses, provided they were not too old, in which case they went to the knacker's yard.

Amazingly, the last coach to carry mail in the British Isles was the

Duchess of Gordon, which made the daily journey between Kingussie and Fort William in Scotland right up until the summer of 1914. It had survived because the railway had not penetrated that far and so still did its daily run, carrying passengers and provisions as well as the mail, along one of the roughest routes for many a mile. The extension of the railway beyond Fort William heralded the impending fate of the famous old coach, and one of its last jobs before it gave way to a Commer charabanc was to carry soldiers to Tulloch. The Kingussie to Fort William road was known as the royal route because first Queen Victoria and Prince Albert, then the new king, Edward VII, had often used it when staying at nearby Laggan. Many times His Majesty's car with the royal standard on it had pulled into the side to let the coach through. Such was the rule of the road; everything gave way to the mail. Sadly, her last run on 1 July 1914 was mourned by few; instead attention was focused on the new motorbus. James Gillie, the coachman, ironically found a new job at a garage serving petrol to the very bus that had put him out of work, and the coach stood outside the Duke of Gordon inn at Kingussie until it fell to bits. Afterwards, local poeple recalled with amusement the notice that used to appear in the newspapers: 'The Duchess will leave the Duke of Gordon at nine every morning, God willing.'

Some coachmen and guards found employment on the railways that had originally deprived them of a job, but many, like Harry Littler of the Southampton Telegraph, were unable to adapt and died unemployed and embittered. Others became landlords of inns, or omnibus- or cab-drivers, and a few fortunate ones became the private coachmen of wealthy patrons who valued their vast experience and skill. Joe Walton, once driver of the Cambridge Star, became a bank messenger, and others found jobs as grooms or porters, while still more ended up in the workhouses, destitute and disheartened. Dick Vickers, who had once driven the Holyhead Mail, tried farming but went bankrupt and eventually killed himself, and Charlie Holmes, driver of the Old Blenheim, committed suicide by jumping into the Thames. But according to Colonel Corbett, in *An Old Coachman's Chatter*, 1890, 'The larger part died off rapidly. They were never a long-lived class of men.'

Although the coming of the railways was the kiss of death for coaching, the introduction of this new fast and economic form of transport was vital for industrial expansion, and horse-drawn transport in Britain reached its heyday during Queen Victoria's reign. More horses than ever before were needed to cope with the great rise in trade and inner-city communications, and by 1900 there were over three hundred thousand horses in London alone – and that was only a tenth of the horses in the whole country. While railways provided the most convenient method of long-distance travel, everything else depended on horse power, or did until the internal combustion engine was introduced. In 1885 a petrol-driven tricycle was exhibited by Edward Butler of Newbury at the International Inventions Exhibition in London, and the following year the Germans were advertising their four-wheeled motor car. Magnus Volk, the managing director of the Brighton Electric Railway, patented an electric dogcart in 1888, the same year as a Scottish veterinary surgeon invented the pneumatic tyre, and by 1895 Frederick Lanchester had built the first British petrol-driven motor car. The innovations were accepted cautiously but with a certain sense of inevitability. Even cyclists were looked upon with disdain, until the Prince of Wales began patronizing the sport and made it fashionable.

Some long-established upper-class families clung obstinately to their traditions and continued to ride in carriages as if defying progress, but all around them the changes were becoming dramatic and swift. Motor vans replaced the tradesmen's carts, private motor cars replaced the broughams and victorias, and even the hansom cabs that had been such a part of city streets began disappearing in the face of competition from motorized taxi-cabs. In 1903 there were still seven thousand five hundred hansoms in daily use in London; eleven years later there were only two hundred. Some of the cab drivers, like Alec Mitchell who had been employed by a jobmaster for forty-three years, found work as chauffeurs, but others, like Henry Upton of Kingston, felt too old to try new jobs and committed suicide. Before he died, Upton wrote, 'Cab work has broken my heart. It is no good. I know it will be starvation for the next six months. Was out for twelve hours on Sunday for one shilling and threepence. I can't stand it any longer.' (*Daily Express*, 18 November 1912.) The sad predicament of the remaining cabmen and the condition of their horses resulted in the formation of a Horse and Drivers' Aid Committee in 1912 'to equip and provide suitable horsedrawn vehicles for those cab drivers too old to learn to drive motors'. The drivers were also to be guaranteed a weekly wage of one pound. The Committee's good intentions were as short-lived as the hansom cabs, which had soon disappeared for ever.

Many of the coach-building firms either closed or began building car bodies instead. The American company of Studebaker was one such firm. Mulliners of Liverpool, Northampton and London started in business as pack-horse proprietors and then ran the Northampton mail coach before turning to carriage building. In 1897 they began automobile body-building, which they still carry out for Rolls-Royce today. Holland and Holland, who were famous for their coaches, were taken over by Thrupp and Maberly who in turn merged with Rootes Motors in 1925. A great many small coach builders became garages specializing in repair work, but the majority simply closed. The well-known London firm of Shanks and Co. staged a farewell party at their premises in Great Queen Street at which they burnt all their valuable plans and drawings on a bonfire in the courtyard. With the coach builders went the harness makers, the blacksmiths and farriers, and the shoeblacks, who, with all the manure in the streets, did a roaring trade polishing the shoes of smart pedestrians.

Many of the harness breeds of horses suffered as a result of mechaniza-tion, for breeders saw little future for their horses with the introduction of the railways and the end of the coaching era in sight. The depression in agriculture in the mid-nineteenth century was the final straw which persuaded many farmers to abandon horse-breeding altogether. Those breeds which survived the bleak years which spanned two world wars tended to be ride-and-drive breeds, versatile enough to find employment as artillery horses, hunters or general riding horses when their services in harness were no longer required. The Morgan horse of America, the Dutch Gelderlander and the Holstein and Hanoverian breeds of Germany all adapted to avoid extinction, but other breeds like the famous Yorkshire Coach Horse and the Norfolk Trotter from which it was descended, merged with other breeds and were lost. In his *Rural Economy of Norfolk*, published in 1795, Marshall mentioned 'the active breed of horse which could not only trot but gallop', one of the most influential stallions being Phenomenon, who was reckoned to be 'at that time the best stallion in England. In height 15 hands 2 inches, on well formed short legs, good feet, deep girth, quarter symmetrical, full of courage, with wonderfully all-found true action.' The Hackney horse, another descendant of the Norfolk Trotter, and the Hackney pony, a separate breed produced by crossing native pony mares with a pony stallion of Norfolk Trotter ancestry, maintained their popularity on both sides of the Atlantic, as the sport of showing Hackneys in harness never went out of fashion. Sir Walter Gilbey, writing about the Hackney in *The Harness Horse*, 1898, described it as having 'shape, action, courage, manners, staying power, and soundness. What would you more?' In the opinion of many, the Hackney was the supreme harness horse, and the Hackney–Welsh Cob cross, or London Cob as it was known in the trade, was a favourite type with the London tradesmen who favoured a fast, flashy type of horse.

The pony breeds, of which Britain had more than any other country, fared little better during the recession than their larger contemporaries, and although some, like the Shetland of northern Scotland and the Connemara from the west coast of Ireland, came through unscathed because mechanization barely penetrated their native haunts, others, including the Fen pony and the Scottish Galloway, died out.

The heavy breeds of Europe, most of which had evolved from the war horses used to carry men in armour in medieval times, had in theory the poorest chances of survival, for they were essentially draught breeds with little scope for diversifying. On the Continent, in areas with a rural economy, breeds like the Ardennes are still used to this day for general agricultural work, and the trade in horse meat for human consumption has for many years provided a ready and consistent market for animals of size and substance. Entires of heavy horse breeds are kept at many of the national studs in France solely for the breeding of meat animals. In Britain, a few devotees have continued to use Clydesdales, Shires and Suffolk Punches on the land in preference to tractors, justifying their preferences on account of the economic viability of horses and the fact that hoofs do less damage to the land than tyres. In forestry, a draught horse can often work, hauling timber, on densely wooded slopes that would be inaccessible to a tractor, and the breweries have always been aware of the advertising value of a horse-drawn dray, which on local runs can generally undercut the running cost of a motorized delivery wagon. The upsurge of interest in showing heavy horses in hand or in harness classes has helped to popularize the breeds with the general public, and the keen interest in trade harness classes and draught competitions, which are especially popular in America, should ensure these breeds of an optimistic future.

Within a matter of a few years the horse population was drastically reduced and thousands of beautiful carriages became suddenly unwanted and were destroyed along with their harness and lamps. One North Country coach builder, the late Mr Birkett of Penrith, recounted in an interview how his firm dismantled old vehicles to use the parts for repairing the last remaining carriages owned by members of the older generation and sent to them for servicing. It was cheaper to do this than make the new parts. Some wheelwrights found a sideline in breaking up the wheels they had in stock and selling the spokes to farmers for ladder rungs, while the axles and other metal parts went for scrap. Fortunately, some vehicles were left discarded in the back of barns and country coach houses to be discovered later, but thousands more were left in fields and yards to rot away.

The picture was the same in America, although because of the immense size of the country, horse-drawn transport survived to a later date in isolated areas not linked by the railways. In the cities like New York trolleys took the place vacated by horse-drawn cabs, and the elegant carriages of previous generations which had turned heads in Central Park now looked outdated alongside the sporty motor cars and electric-powered broughams of a new generation. With the demise of the family coachman, a new class of employee, the coachman/chauffeur, who could drive a car as well as a horse, made his appearance. As well as the handful of purists who believed that the motor car was merely a dangerous fad which would soon go out of fashion again, there were religious sects like the Amish of Pennsylvania who to this day shun motorized transport in favour of the horse. During the 1920s and 30s when it seemed that few people in the States were interested in driving horses, the Amish prevented the skilled work of making harness and building vehicles from dying out altogether, with the result that when the driving renaissance took place a few decades later the Amish found their skills very much in demand.

In Australia, among the last draught horses to go were the heavy horses, descendants of Clydesdales imported during the 1850s, which were used to haul the huge loads of wool from the sheep farms to the towns. The teams consisted of as many as twenty-six horses, and the men who handled them were, in the words of one historian, 'the last of a hard-bitten breed'. Harness racing surprisingly never lost its popularity in either Australia or America.

In Poland, Hungary and other eastern European countries where horse breeding has been a national tradition for centuries, horse-drawn farm transport never really became obsolete, and it survives today alongside tractors and wagons on the large commune farms where horses are still bred in large numbers. Ireland, being another great horse-breeding country, hung on to its horse-drawn transport long after the infiltration of the railways. The Bianconi cars survived because the services they provided were tailored to fit in with the trains, and thirty years into the steam age in 1861 their proprietor, Carlo Bianconi, still employed more than 900 horses and covered 4,000 miles of road. The importance of the horse was waning, however, and many of the men who had driven the 'Bians' lived to see the end of commercial horse-drawn transport in Ireland.

The jobmasters were among the first to realize that the horse and carriage was doomed, and many went into operating strings of motorized taxi-cabs or hiring out motor cars complete with chaffeurs (some of whom had been the cab drivers and grooms of better days). The big forage firms began diversifying their business interests to include dealing in such commodities as potatoes or coal, and the vast stables in which work horses had been kept were altered into warehouses or workshops. Many present-day railway warehouses were once stables. Coach houses were soon adapted into garages, and if extra space was needed for the new and valuable motor cars, the beautiful mahogany stall partitions were ripped out of the stables and the doors widened to accommodate motors. In the streets, petrol pumps began replacing the stone drinking troughs and, in the words of one old ostler, 'the old days were over'.

Chapter 10
Revival and its problems

The war years saw a temporary revival in driving when, with fuel rationed, the pony and trap came back into its own for a brief spell. The coaching amateurs had never given up, and since 1860 had, either privately or in syndicates, run a number of subscription coaches on the old stage-coach roads. The London-to-Brighton road was a favourite route for the amateur sportsmen, whose number included such notable figures as the Duke of Beaufort, Colonel Armitage and Mr Chandos Pole, and their Old Berkeley, Tally-Ho, Venture and Vivid coaches became a familiar sight during the summer months. A few Americans had joined in as well, the most celebrated being the wealthy industrialist, Albert Vanderbilt, who crossed over to England in 1908 with eighty coach horses and became one of the best-known of the pre-war revivalists. On the Continent, in 1883 two English amateurs ran a coach from Pau to Lourdes, a distance of twenty-five miles, and there were a few revival coaches running in Ireland, including several out of Dublin. More recently a Dutchman, Mr Van der Touw, helped to keep the traditions of the road alive by driving his coach from Istanbul to Rotterdam, a distance of 2,175 miles, in thirty-nine days.

The Coaching Club, which was formed in 1871, helped to sustain the interest, and the regular meets which were held in Hyde Park made a marvellous spectacle and played a not insignificant part in interesting the new generation in the art of driving horses. Nevertheless, few people expected driving to survive in any form after the Second World War, but the coaching amateurs were resilient, and in the words of Dick Hunt: 'The curtain was rung down by the war, the death of old friends, roads unsuitable for horses, people careering to and fro without sympathy, manners or love of the beautiful; hotel stables turned into engine sheds and yet, with all these handicaps, it seems that the old game will die hard.' There were even 'a number of new comers and there still remained quite a few old timers'. The example was also set, on a lower scale, by those farmers who retained heavy horses in preference to tractors and by those tradesmen who used horses and carts instead of motor vans and small wagons. Even so, an immense wealth of knowledge had been discarded along with the last of the Edwardian coachmen and ostlers and it was to ensure that the history and art of driving were not lost completely that in 1956 the British Driving Society was formed. Lectures, demonstrations and rallies were organized in different parts of the country and the response was overwhelming. The membership grew until it ran into thousands, and other regional clubs and organizations were set up, abroad as well as in Great Britain, as driving was rediscovered not as a means of transport but as a leisure activity.

The upsurge of interest gave the few remaining wheelwrights and harness makers a new lease of life and the old skills began to be revived as original vehicles were unearthed from their places of storage and put back on the roads. With few professional restorers available to undertake work, many amateurs were obliged at least partially to refurbish their own vehicles, and with the exception of highly skilled work such as the replacement of wheel spokes and felloes, which had to be left to craftsmen, many achieved commendable results.

Bodywork restoration

Before any restoration work is done on a vehicle, it should be carefully dismantled and all metal parts sent to be shot-blasted to remove rust, then zinc-sprayed to discourage them from rusting again. Spring leaves which are badly corroded, brittle or damaged should be replaced, as should any bolts or shackles which are worn. Commercial motor-spring manufacturers will often oblige for one-off orders, and it is a good idea to keep a few spare leaves in stock in case of breakages. If the dashboard and mudguards are leather-covered, the frames should be shot-blasted, zinc-painted and after a top coat of paint sent to a saddler's to be recovered. A good saddler will also be able to replace the leather on the ends of the shafts and where the breeching dees screw on, as well as recovering the head of a hooded vehicle. Usually, if a vehicle has stood neglected for many years, it is the wheels that will have suffered most, and it is well worth the expense of asking a knowledgeable wheelwright to check the wheels over and make good any defective parts. Often it is only the felloes nearest the ground when the vehicle was stored which need replacement, but sometimes the damp will have spread to the spokes and caused rotting there too. Woodworm can be effectively dealt with using one or other of the new insecticides, and provided the damage done is not excessive the wood should not need renewing. If the vehicle was standing with its shafts resting on the ground, check the shaft ends and also further up where they are attached to the vehicle for soundness, as well as for cracks which old paint could hide. All brass or nickel fittings, including shaft furniture, whip sockets and wheel-hub caps should be removed and stored in labelled bags along with their screws. Inevitably, the upholstery will be beyond redemption and in need of renewing but sometimes the original horsehair cushions can be recovered and rebuttoned.

The most time-consuming part of restoration concerns the woodwork, which should be stripped right down using paint stripper and a scraper or piece of glass followed by sandpaper. Blow lamps can leave scorch marks, and electric sanders can cause ridges and grooves unless very carefully used. Any unsound or damaged wood revealed by the stripping process should be renewed, and a liberal coat of clear wood preservative is a good measure on old dried-out wood.

The aim of the initial coats of paint is to fill the grain of the wood and provide a smooth, even surface for the subsequent coats. Several thin coats of aluminium primer, with light sanding in between, are ideal, and these should be followed by coat after coat of undercoat until an absolutely smooth surface is achieved ready for the top coat. Each coat of undercoat must be allowed to dry completely before being lightly sanded prior to the next. A warm, dry and dust-free room is essential for applying the top coats – as many as will give the required finish and depth of colour. Lining out the shafts, wheels and springs is a highly skilled job demanding great patience and a steady hand. Special brushes are used, called lining pencils, with short wooden handles and long bristles which help to keep the lines straight as well as acting as a good reservoir for paint. Quite satisfactory results can also be obtained with patent lining devices which resemble large fountain pens with paint wheels at the end instead of nibs. Finally, one or two coats of clear varnish to protect the paintwork should be applied, then the vehicle can be reassembled ready for the road. If the vehicle is to be stained and varnished instead of painted, care will have to be exercised to ensure that any new wood blends in with the old, as a coat of varnish can change the colour of wood.

Harness restoration

Old harness which has hung for years in an outhouse or stable should be rubbed over with a damp cloth then treated with either harness oil or saddle soap to soften it. Corroded buckle tongues, rotted stitching and cracked or perished leather should be carefully looked for and any defective or dubious parts sent to a reputable saddler for repair. The purchase of old harness which may look quite smart and yet be liable to break on account of its age is a poor investment, as well as a potential source of danger.

Lamps

Carriage and trap lamps come in a variety of shapes and sizes, from the enormous and ornate lamps with engraved glass panes for formal carriages to simple square examples for more humble turnouts. Old lamps can be stripped down, cleaned and repainted successfully at home, but broken panes of glass and corroded panels and stems are a job for a lamp restorer, of which there are now several. Most lamps are fuelled by candles which are housed in the stem under the lamp. The tip of the candle burns through a

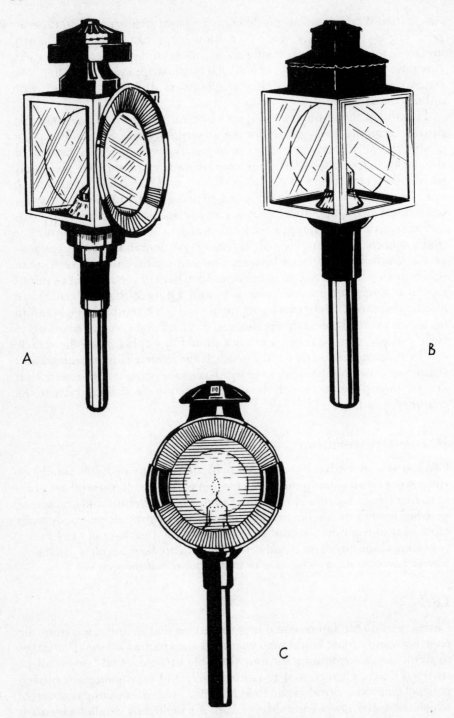

Figure 9 Carriage lamps: *A* oval-faced lamp, *B* square lamp, *C* rear lamp.

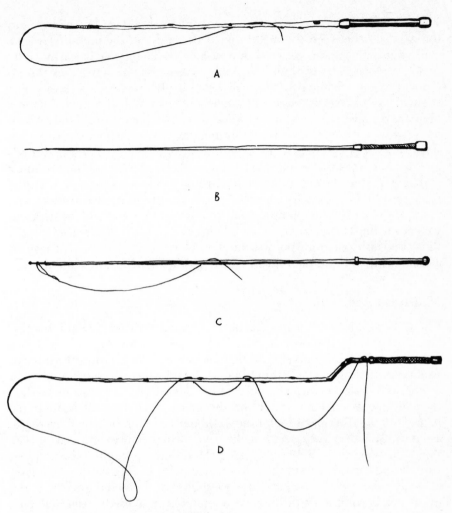

Figure 10 Driving whips: *A* bow-top holly whip, *B* American buggy whip, *C* Continental drop-thong whip, *D* dog-leg four-in-hand whip.

raised aperture in the floor of the lamp and as it burns a spring under the candle expands to push it upwards. The candle is lit by means of a door at the back of the lamp and the candles are renewed by opening the lamp and releasing the catch securing the stem, which then slides down and out. In some cheaper lamps the stems are secured by a simple screw thread.

Whips

A whip should be carefully selected for size and suitability. Traditionally, whips were made from a springy wood such as holly, hickory, lancewood or blackthorn, although whalebone was also used. The thong of plaited white leather, culminating in a short silk lash, is bound with black thread to the stock of the whip through a hollow goose quill to obtain the bowed top, and the handpart between the metal cap at the end and the metal ferrule or collar is usually leather-covered. A well-balanced whip will lie easily in the hand, whereas a badly balanced whip will cause the wrist and thumb muscles to ache. Some people prefer a dog-leg whip (which is shaped like the hind leg of a dog with two right-angle bends), in the belief that it balances better and prevents rainwater trickling up the driver's sleeve. Holly which has grown on stony ground is best for making whips, as it will have grown slowly and be consequently stronger, and straight evenly tapering second-growth shoots of six to seven years of age are best. The stick should be hung with a weight at the end to prevent warping until well seasoned, then the bark should be carefully removed prior to staining, varnishing and mounting with a leather handle, quill and thong. The length of the stick will vary according to the size of the horse being driven – from 3 ft 6 in. with a 4-ft thong and lash for a small pony turnout, to 5 ft with a 12-ft thong and lash for a team whip. The measurements for drop-thong whips are similar.

Maintenance

The working life of carriages, harness and ancillary driving equipment is largely dependent on how it is maintained and cared for. After a vehicle has been used, the floor mats should be removed and shaken and the interior swept out, then the vehicle should be washed down with cold water and a sponge and dried off with chamois leather. Dried-on mud must be washed off with plenty of cold water, or the gritty particles will scratch the paintwork. Leather parts including dashboards should be wiped over with a damp cloth and very occasionally given a light oiling; otherwise they should be polished with boot blacking. Metal fittings ought to be polished with liquid metal polish then burnished with a soft cloth. Axletrees, especially those of the mail axle design, should be greased regularly, and if the wheels become loose through wear a temporary remedy can be effected by cutting and fitting leather washers to the back of the wheel hubs. The vehicle should be stored in an airy, shaded building away from manure heaps, as the ammonia can crack or discolour the paintwork or varnish, as can extremes of temperature, dampness or direct sunlight. The shafts of two-wheeled vehicles should be supported on trestles and the wheels should be spun regularly when not in use, so that the same part of the wheel is not always in contact with the ground. Leather hoods should be left up, as closed or 'struck' hoods are liable to crack along the folds.

Harness should be wiped over with a damp cloth after use to remove mud, grease and sweat. A light oiling at regular intervals will keep the leather supple, although only as much oil as the leather can easily absorb should be applied, or the surface will become too greasy to polish. Boot polish and vigorous brushing will give a good top-shine. Patent leather can be cleaned with the top of the milk on a cloth or a proprietory patent leather cleaner, and metal fittings should again be polished with liquid metal polish

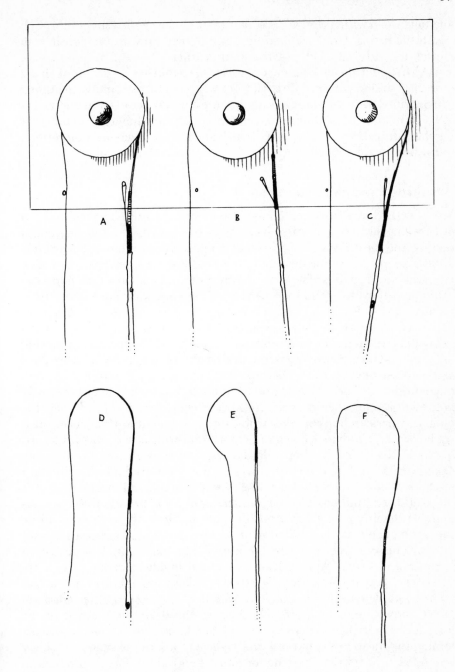

Figure 11 How to hang a driving whip on a whip reel: *A* correctly hung whip, *B* & *C* incorrectly hung whips, *D* thong of a correctly hung whip, *E* & *F* thongs of incorrectly hung whips.

and burnished with a cloth. Pieces of leather or card with a slit cut through which the fitting can be slipped for cleaning will prevent the polish from scratching and dulling the surrounding leather.

Whips should always be hung on reels to keep the shepherd's-crook shape at the top and to prevent the stick from warping. Occasionally, the thong can be wiped over with saddle soap, but the old practice of chalking thongs to keep them white should not be emulated. Lamps should be polished at regular intervals and the interiors, which are usually silver-plate on copper, burnished to aid reflection.

Breaking horses to harness

Since horses were first domesticated 4,000 years ago, innumerable methods of breaking horses to harness have been tried, with varying degrees of success, and the driving revivalists had to reassess these methods, bearing in mind the types of driving for which harness horses were now required. The jobmasters and dealers of what might posthumously be called the horse age could not afford to spend long periods of time breaking horses, and their method was quick and uncompromising. The young horse was simply harnessed alongside an older, experienced and trustworthy horse called a 'schoolmaster' in a skeleton break and made to go. In the early morning light, many city streets witnessed fierce battles between the horsebreakers and their unwilling pupils. Their method of breaking, although successful, often produced sullen or ill-tempered animals, but such faults were hardly noticed at a time when horses were worked commercially. J.S. Rarey, the famous American horsebreaker who came to England in 1858, astonished the horse world with a spectacular demonstration of his skill, and advertised his 'new theory of taming wild horses, which is the result of many experiments, and a thorough investigation and trial of the different methods of horsemanship now in use'. After breaking in Lord Dorchester's thoroughbred stallion, Cruiser, which had been pronounced 'an un-tamable devil' and a zebra from the zoo, he then offered to teach one thousand people his method of breaking for a fee of ten guineas each. Not only was he soon oversubscribed, but two of his eager pupils were Queen Victoria and Prince Albert. Rarey's method involved making the horse powerless by means of a series of leg straps, pulleys and hobbles until he had gained complete mastery. *The Army Manual of Horsemanship, Equitation and Driving* advocated a compromise between the dramatic method of the jobmasters and the modern system of breaking, which involves accustoming the horse to the harness and vehicle in a series of stages. It sagely reminded trainers that 'instruction must be gradual and continuous to produce the trained draught horse'.

These days most horses and ponies being trained for harness work are already broken to ride, so most of the initial training, including lunging and long-reining, will already have been done, and the proceeding steps, which should be gradual with progress halted until each lesson has been thoroughly learned, will in the first stages be more in the form of revision than new ground. Few riding horses will object to being lunged with a roller or pad on, but many will object strongly when a crupper is buckled on for the first time by clamping their tails down and kicking, which is a natural reaction. Should this happen, the pupil should be made to go forward regardless. Once acceptance of the crupper has been established, the back band, belly band and tugs can be fixed to the pad and the breeching put on, with the breeching straps buckled by means of leather extensions to the tugs to prevent the breeching from sliding up should the horse start to kick. In due course the collar, hames and traces can be put on, with the latter slipped through the tugs and coiled around themselves and the breeching straps now buckled through the trace hook slots in the end of the traces. This will accustom the horse to the feel of breeching pressure on his quarters. It is a good idea to fasten the hame terrets on the collar to the pad terrets with a leather strap, to prevent the collar from sliding down the horse's neck should he lower his head. Lunging with the harness on will not only get the horse used to the feel of harness, but will teach him basic obedience as well. Always use an open bridle for these early lessons, and give consistent verbal commands – walk on, trot on, steady, halt, etc., which will be used later when he is actually driven in a vehicle. The horse must know your voice and respond to it, because in driving, the voice, reins and whip are the only aids we can use. Care should be taken to ensure that the harness fits comfortably and does not rub or pinch the horse.

Long-reining is an important part of the training process, as driving itself is really only an extension of long-reining. Initially, most trainers lunge the horse using two reins, the inside rein giving direct control while the outside rein lies loosely across the horse's back. If the horse is liable to kick as a result of the outside long-rein across his back and, later, around his quarters a lunge-rein on to a cavesson will give additional control without interfering with the horse's mouth. For the first few lessons, changes of rein should be made by stopping the horse, reversing the position of the reins, then quietly setting him off in the opposite direction, but as the horse progresses to being driven from behind, as it would be in a vehicle, it should be possible to turn the horse across the school using light, even pressure on the inside rein, which, as the pressure is transferred to the other rein to complete the manoeuvre, becomes the outside rein. It is important to ease the rein pressure as soon as a movement is completed and to use the reins in unison, slackening one rein when applying pressure to the other when changing direction or driving figures or circles. As soon as the pupil has got to the stage of being long-reined from behind rather than from the central area of a lunging arena, the reins should pass from the bit rings through the shaft tugs on the belly band to the driver, but not through the terrets, as this minimizes control should the horse play up. Time spent teaching a horse to long-rein is time well spent. A knowledgeable assistant who will, if necessary, lead the horse on in the early lessons is invaluable, and as in all stages of breaking a horse, everything should be done in a quiet workmanlike manner with the minimum of fuss or impatience. The horse should be taught to walk on, turn in either direction, complete simple figures and halt calmly before being taken out on to the roads to widen his experience and introduce him to the hazards of motorized traffic.

Despite the words of the infamous J.S. Rarey, who advised his pupils, 'Always use a bridle without blinds when you are breaking a horse to harness,' very few horses are driven in open bridles. Blinkers prevent horses being frightened by the sight of moving wheels behind them, the whip being used to give traffic signals, umbrellas being raised, etc. The pupil should be given plenty of time to get used to blinkers and being long-reined in them, and it is at this point when the driver can no longer be seen that the benefits of teaching the horse verbal commands will be realized.

The pupil should be unperturbed about the reins touching his hindquarters and legs and now ready to learn to pull. The full set of harness should be put on the horse with the addition of two lengths of rope which are attached to the trace ends, thereby extending the length of the traces about nine or ten feet. As the horse is driven on the long-reins, an assistant pulls back on the extended traces so that the horse not only has to pull from the collar but also gets used to the feel of the traces against its legs. The next stage is to pull an actual load, and a large old tyre, log or small sledge is ideal, the traces being fastened to a swingletree attached to the load with a short length of rope or chain. A trace bearer over the horse's loins reduces the risk of the horse getting a leg over a trace when turning. Some people like to work their young horses in chain harrows prior to being harnessed into a vehicle, and this is a good idea as it also accustoms the pupil to noise from behind. Failing this, someone pushing a wheelbarrow or dragging a chain behind the horse will serve the same purpose.

The final stage of breaking a horse to drive is to harness him into the vehicle, and this should only be undertaken when the horse has successfully learnt all the previous lessons and is obedient to the voice and reins. Some trainers give their horses an introduction to shafts by long-reining them with two thin poles slipped through the tugs and breeching and secured there with little leather straps or string. The ideal vehicle to break a horse into is a skeleton breaking cart, a specially built two-wheeled vehicle with a metal bridge over the extra-long shafts to carry the reins clear of the horse's back. Unfortunately, such vehicles are now rare, but any strong sound vehicle can be used providing that it offers easy access to the driver and is not too heavy. The harness should be very strong and supple so that all buckles can be easily undone, and a kicking strap from shaft to shaft over the horse's loins to prevent it getting its hindquarters up to kick is a wise precaution. A strong headcollar should be worn under the bridle with a lead-rope of at least six to eight feet. One knowledgeable assistant is essential and two are even better. Before being 'put to' for the first time, the horse should be quietly worked on the lunge or under saddle to settle it, and if the weather is windy or very wet it is prudent to abandon the project until a more favourable day. If the horse is uneasy, facing him against a wall to harness him to the vehicle may encourage him to stand, but it also means that he will have to turn as soon as he moves off, which is not always such a good idea.

To 'put to', one person should hold the horse by the reins or lead-rope while the other two people quietly wheel the vehicle up from behind and slip the shafts through the tugs. The traces should be fastened to the tracehooks or swingletree quickly and the use of strong cord at the trace ends tied in quick-release knots may make unharnessing easier, especially if the horse needs to be unharnessed in a hurry. The breeching straps should be buckled to the shafts next so that there is no danger of the vehicle rolling forward and striking the horse's hocks, as nothing is more likely to frighten a young horse and teach it to kick. The belly band should be buckled fairly tight to prevent the shafts from moving at all, as this could easily upset an inexperienced horse. Once he is harnessed in and everything has been checked over, the driver should position himself on the near side of the horse just in front of the vehicle and holding the reins. One assistant should lead the horse and the other assistant should help by walking on the offside and gently pulling or pushing the shaft to left or right to aid the horse in turning the vehicle. A flat open field is most suitable for these first drives, which should be kept fairly short – no longer than ten minutes, as the horse can soon begin to tire and ache, particularly if the vehicle is heavy or the field wet and muddy. When the horse will do in the vehicle what he did in long-reins, the driver can mount the vehicle, and this should be done when in motion so that the horse does not have to move a stationary deadweight. An assistant can join the driver in the vehicle in due course, although a 'gypsy line' or long cord from the horse's head to the assistant in the vehicle is advisable in case of mishaps. As the length of the drives is increased, steady trotting may be introduced, and some hill work can be included. Steep downhill gradients should be avoided until the pupil has gained more experience, and reining back should not be attempted until free forward movement has been achieved. Schooling a horse in harness is a slow process. The old dealers used to say that it took a season to make a riding horse but several years to make a driver.

Correct harnessing

No horse can be expected to go well between shafts unless the harness fits comfortably with each part performing its function correctly. When harnessing, the horse should be tied up or held by an assistant using a headcollar and lead-rope. The collar goes on first, but before putting it on it should be widened by placing one's knee against the lining and pulling upwards to temporarily stretch it laterally. This helps it to go over the horse's head

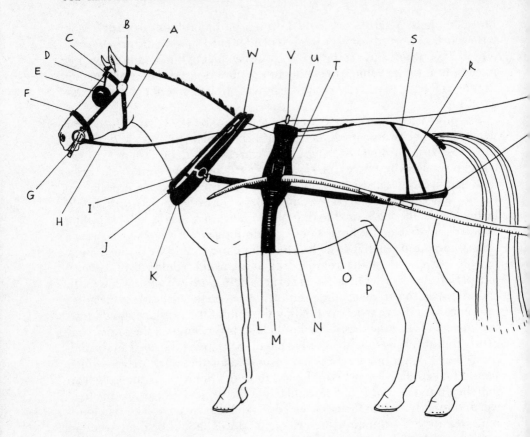

Figure 12 Single driving harness: *A* throat latch or lash, *B* headpiece, *C* browband, *D* blinkerstay, *E* blinker, *F* noseband, *G* Liverpool driving bit, *H* rein, *I* hames, *J* bottom hame strap or hame chain, *K* collar, *L* girth, *M* belly band, *N* tug, *O* trace, *P* shaft, *Q* breeching, *R* loin strap, *S* back strap and crupper, *T* pad, *U* saddle, *V* terret, *W* top hame strap.

without pressing on its eyes, which would soon make the horse headshy. Turning the collar upside down so that the widest part is at the top, it should be carefully slipped over the horse's head. Once past the poll, the hames, fastened together by the bottom hame strap only and with the traces attached and looped around themselves, are lifted into place, and their top strap buckled before the collar is turned right way up, at the narrowest part of the horse's throat and in the direction the mane lies. It can then be slid down on to the shoulders and the top hame strap tightened so that the hames are held firmly in their groove in the collar. There are many types of collars designed for different uses, but whichever kind is used, the collar should lie flat on the horse's shoulders with room to get two fingers between the sides of the collar and the neck and one's hand between the bottom of the collar and the windpipe. When in draught the collar should neither tip nor

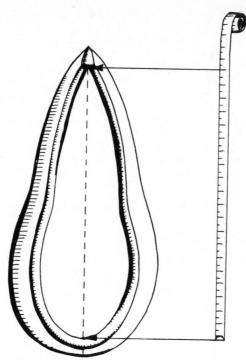

Figure 13 How to measure a driving collar.

rock. The making of collars is a highly skilled trade and collar- and harness-makers were generally quite separate concerns. Collars should be checked periodically for fit, as a pony which takes a 19-in. collar at the beginning of the season may need a 20-in. or even 21-in. collar later in the year when its neck has muscled up. Breast or Dutch collars are much easier to fit, lighter in weight and can be used on horses of different sizes, but they are only suitable for light work as the weight is less evenly distributed than with a neck collar, and breast collars are more liable to cause collar sores.

The pad, complete with belly band, tugs, crupper and breeching, is put on next, a little way back while the tail is slipped through the crupper, then lifted forward and girthed up. Care should be taken to see that there is no hair trapped under the tail, as this could rub causing soreness, and the pad should be well clear of the withers and not pressing on the spine. The girth need not be as tight as on a riding saddle, and the belly band should be loosely buckled for the time being. The reins should be passed through the pad and collar terrets and the loose ends caught up on the collar terrets until the bridle is put on. The handpart ends should be buckled together (buckle rein on nearside), and slipped through the offside pad terret. Lastly, the bridle should be put on and the noseband and throat-latch fastened. The blinkers should fit so that the horse's eyes are behind the centre of them, and should be very carefully adjusted so that the eyes are in no danger of being

Figure 14 Wilson or double-ring snaffle bit.

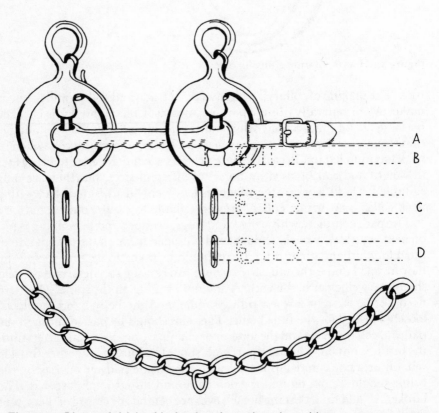

A

B

C

D

Figure 15 Liverpool driving bit showing alternative rein positions.

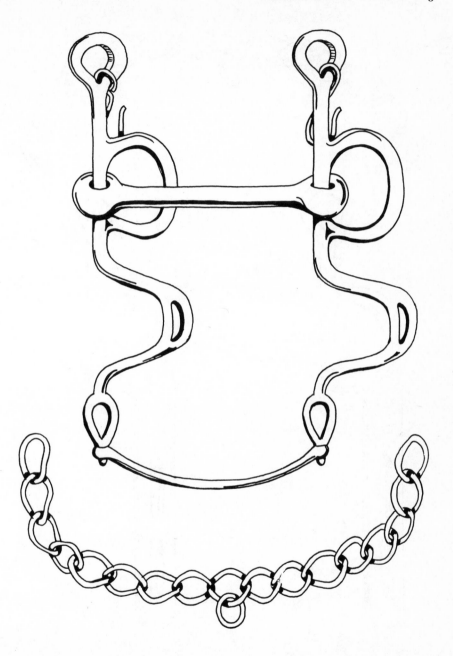

Figure 16 Buxton driving bit.

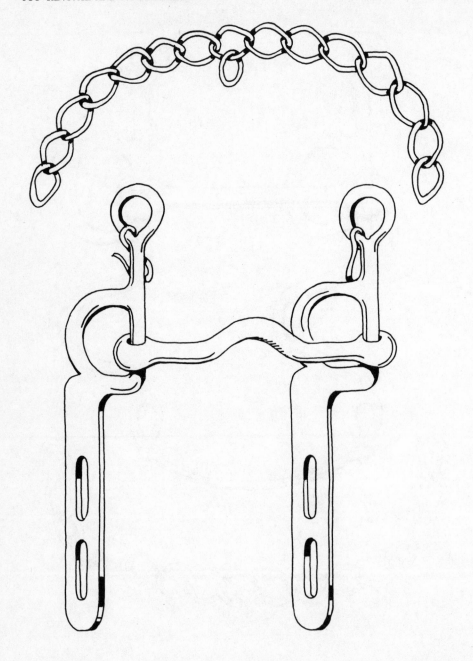

Figure 17 Elbow driving bit.

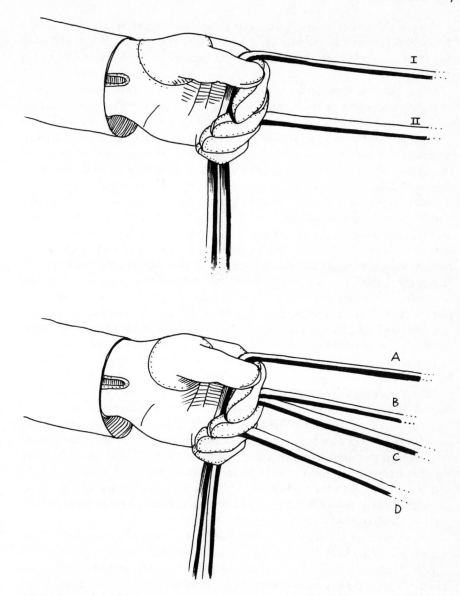

Figure 18 How to hold driving reins: single or pair reins. *I* nearside rein, *II* offside rein.

Figure 19 How to hold driving reins: team or tandem reins. *A* nearside leader(s) *B* offside leader(s) *C* nearside wheeler(s) *D* offside wheeler(s).

rubbed or pressed. The headpiece and cheekpieces must be adjusted so that the blinkers cannot bulge out when pressure is applied to the bit, allowing the horse to see behind. Lastly, the reins should be buckled on to the bit rings.

There are innumerable types of driving bits, some with straight mouthpieces, some jointed, others with ports, curb chains, on twisted, rubber or vulcanite mouthpieces, and it is important to find the bit which best suits a particular horse. Drop or grackle nosebands, tongue straps, bearing reins and martingales can all supplement the action of different bits. These days there are four main types of driving bit. The Wilson or driving snaffle has the disadvantage of all bits with jointed mouthpieces in its nutcracker action, but many horses go well in one. The bridle cheekpieces should be buckled to the floating rings and the reins buckled around both rings. Very severe action is effected if the reins are buckled to the outer rings only. The Liverpool driving bit is the most widely used of all curb driving bits, and there are innumerable variations on the basic theme. In addition, the reins can be attached to the bit in different ways to increase or decrease the severity of the action, making this bit suitable for most horses. The Buxton is an ornate-looking bit, rarely used with a single turnout, and usually reserved for formal occasions or the show ring, while the elbow bit is very similar in action to the Liverpool bit except that the angled cheeks are set back to prevent the horse from getting hold of them in his teeth.

When correctly 'put to', the breeching should be loose enough not to impede the horse's movement, but sufficiently tight to keep the vehicle well clear of the horse's hindquarters when going downhill. To achieve proper balance the traces should be adjusted to such a length that when the vehicle is in motion the shaft tugs lie in the middle of the pad, and the belly band should be loose enough to leave sufficient play for the shafts to move up and down slightly. As a four-wheeled vehicle is self-supporting and does not need balancing, this play is unnecessary and Tilbury or French tugs which hold the shafts firmly to the pad are used.

Before slipping the reins out of the pad terret and mounting the vehicle, the whip should check that the harness is correctly adjusted, and the groom or passenger should not mount until the driver is seated and has full control. The reins should be held in the left hand at all times, the nearside rein over the index finger and the offside rein under the middle finger, the right hand being used to assist the left hand when decreasing pace or turning. In some Eastern European countries, the reins are held in both hands as they are for certain types of driving in America and for showing Hackneys in harness, or they are held in one hand but using a leather handle called a 'frog'. A whip should be carried at all times and used by placing the thong between the horse's collar and pad. Striking the horse on the rump with the stock of the whip is likely to encourage the horse to kick.

Chapter 11

Competitive driving

Driving as a recreational sport has been practised in various parts of the world for nearly three centuries and is the foundation upon which most present-day driving flourishes. The combination of man's skill and ingenuity with the strength and stamina of the horse has made competitive driving a popular and sometimes spectacular sport since the days when the Roman Emperor Nero drove in the chariot races at Delphi, and new and specialist forms of driving have been evolved in recent years to meet the demands of present-day competitors eager to participate in this age-old sport.

It was the Greeks who introduced the first competitive driving in the form of chariot racing, and their example was quickly taken up by others, in particular the Romans, who virtually made it a national sport. Organized chariot races were a part of the Olympic games in 776 BC, the year in which the Greeks started to record the winners' names. The races were held in the open air with the two ends of the track marked by wooden posts or heaps of stones. The actual chariots were very light, with small wheels and very wide axles to ensure stability at speed, and the simple rawhide harness was fastened with knots instead of buckles.

Rome had a number of racetracks, including the magnificent Circus Maximus, which measured 600 by 200 metres and had seating for 255,000 spectators. There were twelve starting-stalls at one end of the course and a raised bank in the centre with seven bronze dolphins on top which were used as lap markers. Under the Emperor Augustus twelve races were run each day, but this number was increased to twenty-four by Caligula, and there were races for from two to ten horses driven together. Most of the charioteers were of humble origin, many of them emancipated slaves, but they stood to amass great wealth if successful on the racetrack. Cheating and bad sportsmanship seem to have been quite acceptable and only added to the excitement of the occasion. Accidents were frequent and usually fatal, and the life expectancy of a charioteer was only about twenty-five years. The epitaph for Scorpus, a wealthy and successful charioteer, reads, 'I am Scorpus, the pride of the noisy circus. But alas! short was the time Rome could applaud me; when I reached thrice nine years, I was carried off by a jealous Fate who, counting my victories, believed that I was old.'

The Roman charioteers used to fasten the reins around their waists (a dangerous tradition not practised by the Greeks), and carried a knife with which to cut themselves free in case of accidents. Despite this precaution many unfortunate charioteers were either dragged to their deaths or trampled by the other competitors.

Chariot races were not always held for entertainment; excavations at Stonehenge in Wiltshire have revealed a track where chariots are believed to have been raced as part of the burial rituals. From paintings in the Egyptian tombs we know that fast light chariots were also used for hunting such prey as ostrichs. The eclipse of the Roman Empire saw the demise of chariot racing forever, but harness racing in other forms was to spread rapidly.

Harness or trotting racing, as we know it today, originated in the United States, where a breed of horse, the Standard Bred, was produced specifically for harness races. Based on Thoroughbred, Morgan and Norfolk Trotter blood lines, Standard Bred horses could trot a mile in under two minutes, and most European trotting horses have Standard Bred blood somewhere in their ancestry. Although harness racing has remained the premier spectator horse sport with the American public, trotting tracks are now to be found all over the world, with regular race meetings held to cater for both trotters and pacers (the former moving diagonally, the latter laterally). At first the horses were raced in two- or four-wheeled road carts on the open road, but as the sport developed a new type of low two-wheeled vehicle, built of hickory or tubular steel and called a sulky because of the single seat, was devised. Harness, like the vehicle, is kept to a minimum with a light pad and breast collar, and open bridles usually with an overcheck on to the snaffle bit are frequently used. The drivers wear coloured 'silks' as in ridden racing and a handicapping system is operated at race meetings. In 1938 a horse called Greyhound trotted the mile in 1 minute 55¼ seconds, but an American trotter holds the record at 1 minute 54.8, while a pacer has beaten both trotters with an incredible 1 minute 54 seconds flat.

In Russia harness races on the snow were held, the horses being harnessed to light sleighs and specially shod to give them a grip, while in Switzerland the sport of *skijoering*, or racing over the snow with the drivers on skiis instead of in vehicles, is now very popular at the fashionable resorts.

One of the most distinctive forms of harness racing is American chuck-wagon racing which was devised by Guy Weadlock, a travelling showman, and first held at the Calgary Stampede in Canada in 1923. Now staged at all major American rodeos, the teams consist of a specially constructed canvas covered chuck wagon drawn by four horses, usually Thoroughbred rejects from the racetrack, plus two mounted escorts who have to load the wagon with a kitchen stove and other equipment, then mount and follow the racing chuckwagon through a tight course set out between barrels. At the finishing line the mounted escorts must be level with the wagon.

In Britain, annual agricultural shows with classes for local breeds of livestock including horses had been instigated in many parts of the country early in the nineteenth century, but harness classes did not come until much later. Generally these early show classes were patronized by wealthy stud owners, many of whom employed professional coachmen and showmen, or affluent tradesmen keen to exhibit their fine horses and advertise their firms. Until the First World War gave a premature, if temporary, check to the elegant and privileged sport of showing horses in harness, driving classes had been gaining in popularity, and the coaching marathons at shows like Richmond and Olympia sometimes had as many as twenty entries. Many of the exhibitors were wealthy amateur coachmen who ran road coaches on some of the old stage-coach routes during the summer months for their own sport and to keep the traditions of the road alive. Other competitors included such sportsmen as the American millionaires Alfred G. Vanderbilt and Judge Moore, who would bring over as many as fifty horses from America in order to compete in the harness classes at the large shows like Olympia. Here classes were staged for singles, pairs, tandems, novices and even for gigs and governess cars, as well as the important coaching marathons. One or two lady whips competed at these shows, including Miss Ella Ross and Miss Sylvia Brocklebank. The latter's many wins included the class for 'the quickest change of teams in the ring' at the International Horse Show in London in 1908. Her grooms unharnessed one team from the coach and harnessed another in their place in forty-eight seconds. The ostlers of the celebrated coachman, James Selby, changed teams in forty-seven seconds during a famous feat in 1888 when Selby drove the Old Times coach from London to Brighton and back, a distance of 108 miles, in under eight hours, but this record was beaten in 1963 when the grooms of Sanders Watney's Red Rover coach made the changeover in a time of forty-five seconds.

General points on competing

The criteria by which present-day private driving classes are judged are based on the fundamental rules handed down to us by previous generations who drove horses daily for pleasure and business. The term 'private driving' limits entries to owner-driven vehicles, as opposed to either coachman-driven vehicles like broughams or trade vehicles like butchers' carts, which at some of the larger shows are catered for in special trade classes. Methods of judging vary from country to country. Harness horse classes in America are judged on a points system, which in theory should simplify the job of judging, but in practice insufficient consideration may be given to how the separate parts of the turnout combine to give a pleasing overall effect, with the result that the judge may eventually feel dissatisfied with his own decision.

Generally the qualities by which driving horses are judged are the same as for riding horses, but with special emphasis on strong quarters, good legs

Schedule of classes

TIME	CLASS	DESCRIPTION
10.00 a.m.	1	*Novice driving* – Open to horses or ponies which have not won a first prize in a driving class at the date of entry.
10.45 a.m.	2	*Single harness* – Ponies 14.2 hh. or under driven to a suitable vehicle.
11.30 a.m.	3	*Single harness* – Horses over 14.2 hh. driven to a suitable vehicle.
12.15 p.m.	4	*Trade turnout* – Open.
1.00 p.m.	5	*Pairs and tandems* – Any height driven to a suitable vehicle.
1.45 p.m.	6	*Mountain and moorland* – All animals to be registered in the main section of their respective Breed Society stud book. Part-breds are not eligible for this class. Special rosette for the best of each breed.
2.30 p.m.	7	*Knockout novelty stakes* – Single or pair, any height. Two identical courses of cones and obstacles will be built and competitors will drive against each other in pairs, the winner from each pair to go forward to the final.
3.15 p.m.	8	*Junior whip* – To be driven by a junior eighteen years or under to a suitable vehicle. This class is judged to determine the capabilities of the whip, and particular attention will be paid to dress, turnout and driving procedure. Special rosettes to all entrants.
4.00 p.m.	9	*Exercise vehicle* – Single horse or pony, any height, driven to an exercise vehicle. Pneumatic tyres allowed. Show vehicles and traditional vehicles debarred.
4.30 p.m.	10	*Ride and drive* – Single horse or pony, any height. Competitors will be required to drive into the ring first, give a short driven show then leave the ring and return under saddle to give a ridden show and jump one obstacle of 2′ 6″. This is not against the clock.
5.00 p.m.	11	*Concours d'élégance* – Open. The object of this class is to establish which turnout, in the opinion of the judge, is the most elegant. It will be judged from a distance by an artist and normal judging criteria will not apply. Fancy dress or period costume is not allowed.

The show championship will be judged in the main ring immediately after class 11 and first prize winners from classes 1–6, 8 and 9 will be required.

Figure 20 Specimen schedule for a driving show.

and feet and plenty of depth through the heart. The shoulders may be straighter than would be required in a riding horse, and a slightly common or overlarge head will look less obvious in a driving bridle. A longish back is also less objectionable in a driving horse than in a riding horse. A sensible temperament is a great asset. Exaggerated action is not required, which is why Hackneys are debarred from many private driving classes, but free forward movement at walk and trot with the horse covering the ground is important, as are perfect manners at all times. The old jobmasters always tried to avoid horses with low sweeping action, as a rut or cobble in the road could be enough to bring them down when moving at speed. High-stepping action, on the other hand, was considered wasteful and a compromise was preferred.

The two essentials with harness are that it should be sound and well-fitting. For showing, a full collar is smarter than a breast collar, but if a full collar is used it must be neither too small so that it presses on the windpipe, which could in time cause respiratory troubles, nor so large that it rocks on the horse's shoulders, causing soreness. The harness must be supple and clean, with the furniture or metal fittings well polished. Traditionally, fittings were 'brass for a gentleman, nickel for a cabman', and while brass fittings are preferable in a private driving class and nickel or white metal in a trade class, the important thing is that the fittings on the harness match the fittings on the vehicle, including the lamps. A century ago it was usual to use black harness with the town vehicles which were coachpainted, and brown harness with the country vehicles which were varnished wood, and this rule still applies, although even with black harness the reins should always be tan-coloured as black reins would leave dye stains on the gloves and clothes. Black harness can be made with either plain or patent leather, and although the latter looks very smart when new, it scratches easily and can soon look shabby, whereas plain leather will polish up again and again and retain its smartness for considerably longer. A full set of single private driving harness consists of a bridle, which may have square, round or hatchet-shaped blinkers; a full collar with hames or a breast collar; traces; pad complete with back band and tugs; crupper; breeching; false martingale and reins. A 'false' breeching, which is a strap which fastens between the shafts, is sometimes used in place of a full breeching to display the horse's quarters better.

Pair harness is similar to two sets of single harness in many respects, the main differences being that the collars have a ring or link at the front to take the pole straps which attach to the pole end, and the hame tugs are longer and buckle on to the tug straps on the pad, with the belly band fastened to the two short leather straps which hang from the tug buckles at either side. The trace ends have loops to fasten to the roller bolts on the splinter bar of the vehicle, and breeching is usually used only for driving in hilly country or if the vehicle has no brake. The reins are made with couplings so that the nearside rein controls the near side of each horse and vice versa.

Tandem harness consists of a set of gig harness for the wheeler with the addition of split terrets on the pad – the wheel reins passing through the lower half and the lead reins through the upper – and loops on the underside of the hame tug buckles to take the ends of the leader's traces. The leader's harness is similar to the wheeler's except that there are no back band or tugs on the pad, which has loops on the skirt instead to take the traces, which are about 3 ft longer than on single harness. The leader's reins pass through the terrets on the collar and pad, through rings on the wheeler's bridle rosettes and through the split terrets on the wheeler's pad. Occasionally tandem bars are used, as these reduce the risk of a horse getting a leg over the long lead traces.

The vehicle must not only be sound and roadworthy, in smart order and immaculately clean, it must fit the horse or horses in size as well as type. Horses in single or tandem harness look best in a two-wheeled vehicle. It is possible to drive a pair or even a team to a two-wheeled vehicle using specialized harness, but turnouts harnessed in this way are unusual. The vehicle and type of horse should also be compatible. Cobs and native ponies look best in sporty vehicles like dogcarts or ralli cars, whereas a Hackney or part-bred horse may be better suited to a light skeleton or cut-under gig. Traditional colours for vehicles are black, dark green, navy or maroon, lined in a constrasting colour, although black and yellow has always been a favourite colour for sporting vehicles like dogcarts, and other colour combinations are peculiar to certain countries, like the black and white chaises drawn by Friesian horses which appear at Dutch shows. Garish lining should be avoided and varnished vehicles should not be lined at all. Fawn-coloured upholstery is preferable to dark, which shows up any loose hair from the horses, especially if they are greys. Lamps of a size suitable for the vehicle should be carried, and a small rear lamp may also be fitted to the rear of the vehicle. If the lamp candles are new, they should be lit then blown out, as a candle which has already been lit will light more readily and save time, and everything in a driving class is based on practicality. A box of spares, including a spare rein, trace and hame strap, strong cord, a knife, a hoof pick and a headcollar should be carried. A cylindrical wicker or leather umbrella basket is sometimes strapped to the side of the vehicle, and if one is carried there should be an umbrella in it.

The dress of the driver or 'whip', as he or she is correctly called, is very important. A gentleman should wear a suit, soft leather gloves which fit loosely and a bowler, although for tandem or team driving a top hat is smarter. In wet weather, wool or string gloves give a better grip on damp slippery reins. For lady whips, a discreetly coloured outfit, gloves and a narrow-brimmed hat are most practical. Huge floppy hats, tight skirts, high-heeled shoes and garish colours should be avoided at all costs. A whip should always be carried. The knee rug or apron is worn to keep the clothes clean as well as the wearer warm in cold weather. Beige material, called 'drab' in years gone by, blends well with most colours and does not show the dirt and horsehair as noticeably as a dark colour would. In warm weather, a blue and white 'tattersall' check may be worn but loud or bright colours are quite wrong.

The transportation of horse-drawn turnouts to shows and events can often be a problem. The ideal arrangement is a large wagon into which the horses, vehicle and harness boxes will fit, but for single, pair or tandem turnouts a simple and quite satisfactory answer is a pickup truck on to which the vehicle can be loaded, and a double trailer which is towed behind. It is always advisable to cover the vehicle with a well-secured tarpaulin, as dirt or grit thrown up from the road can ruin paintwork and leather dashboards.

Private driving classes

Private driving classes are sometimes subdivided into single and pair sections, while at some of the larger shows a section for unicorns and teams is also provided, along with classes for novice horses, mountain and moorland ponies, lady whips and so forth. A short road marathon is often incorporated so that the judge may see how the horses go on the open road and in traffic, as well as in the confines of the show ring, where each exhibit will be required to give a brief show to demonstrate basic obedience. The ring steward will advise exhibitors of what is required but usually all turnouts are asked to go around the ring in a clockwise direction, although they may be required to change the rein later and go anti-clockwise at the judge's request. Exhibitors should allow plenty of room between themselves and the turnouts in front and behind, to allow the judge to see them properly. After a few circuits of the ring the steward will call all turnouts into line and the judge will inspect each one in turn before asking each exhibitor to do an individual show. This should comprise walking quietly out of the line, trotting a large figure of eight, or up and down in front of the other horses if space is limited, a halt, and a reinback of no more than four paces. Occasionally the judge may drive the turnouts himself to see how they handle. If a road marathon is included the distance is usually about five miles and the required speed will be about seven miles per hour.

The classification laid out in schedules will vary from show to show, but the wording will probably be something similar to the following:

PRIVATE DRIVING CLASS. Horses or ponies, any height (non-Hackney type), four years old or over, to be driven single, pair or tandem to a suitable vehicle. Commercial vehicles and Hackney show wagons debarred. No marathon.

In American show schedules private driving classes are called pleasure classes and entries are judged on the suitability of the horse/pony to provide a pleasant drive. Exhibits are:

to be shown both ways of the arena at a walk, collected trot, working trot, and trot-on. To stand quietly when asked, and to back readily. Those chosen for a

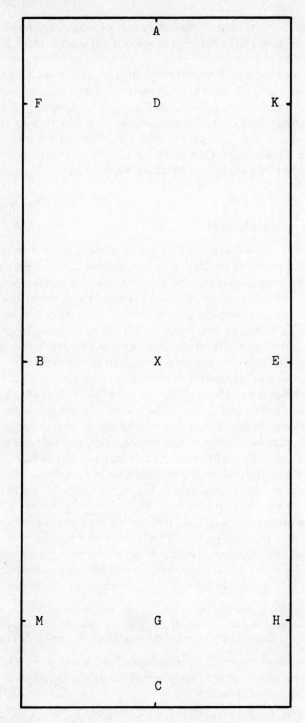

Figure 21 Layout of a dressage arena, 100 x 40 metres.

workout [individual show] may be asked to work both ways of the arena at any gait requested by the judge, and may be asked to perform a figure of eight. Performance, manners and way of going, 70%; condition, fit and appropriateness of harness and vehicle, 20%; and appropriateness and neatness of attire, 10%.

Ride-and-drive classes

Ride-and-drive competitions can take two forms; a speed competition in which the exhibitor must drive a set course of obstacle cones, unharness, saddle up and ride the horse over a series of small jumps, then harness up again to drive the obstacle cones a second time, the fastest competitor winning; or a style competition which is not timed. The latter is judged firstly as a private driving class and secondly as a riding-horse class with one or more optional jumps. A typical classification for a ride-and-drive class in America may read:

> To be shown in harness to a suitable pleasure driving vehicle. To be shown both ways of the arena at a walk, collected trot, working trot and trot-on. To stand quietly, and back readily. To be shown under saddle at a walk, trot and canter, to stand quietly, and back readily. In harness 50%; under saddle 50%.

Timed rides and drives originated from obstacle driving competitions in which the competitor has to negotiate a prescribed course of obstacles, the number of obstacles being proportionate to the dimensions of the arena. After passing the starting line, the competitor proceeds in the shortest possible time through each obstacle to the finish line. Course faults are scored as penalty seconds and added to the competitor's time. The fastest time wins, and ties for first are decided by a drive-off. These classes in turn gave rise to scurries, in which pairs of ponies are driven around a very tight course of obstacle cones against the clock. Special lightweight vehicles with a full front-wheel lock and a low centre of gravity are used for scurries.

Gambler's stakes

Another class in some schedules is the 'gambler's stakes' where each driver has the same amount of time to negotiate as many obstacles as possible. Each obstacle is assigned a point value according to its degree of difficulty, and each driver tries to amass as high a point score as possible in the time allowed. Obstacles may be driven in any order and may be approached from either direction. Each obstacle may be attempted twice, but competitors must attempt a different obstacle before returning for a second try. A signal will sound the end of the time allowed – usually two minutes – and after the signal the competitor must exit through the finish line. At that point the total time on course will be recorded. In the event of equality of points, the fastest time recorded determines the winner.

Reinsmanship

Reinsmanship classes are sometimes included in the schedules of American shows and entries are judged 'primarily on the skill and ability of the driver'. Handling of the reins and whip, control of the horse(s), posture and overall appearance count for 70% of the marks, the other 30% being for condition, fit and appropriateness of harness, vehicle and attire.

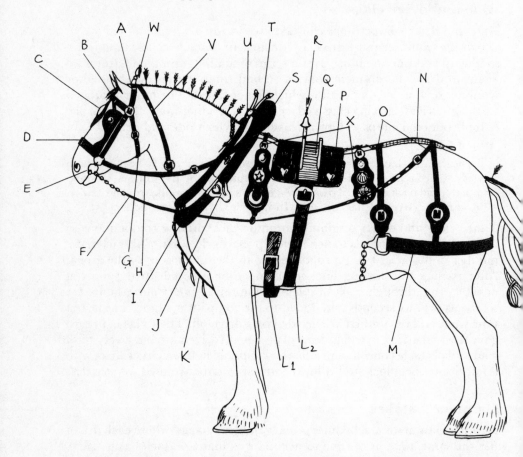

Figure 22 Decorated cart harness: *A* headpiece, *B* browband and winkerstay, *C* face piece or facen (decorative), *D* noseband and blinkers stitched into one piece with no chin strap, *E* bit, *F* rein, *G* throat latch or lash, *H* lead rein/brearing rein, *I* collar, *J* hame hook, *K* breast plate (decorative), *L1* belly band, attached to shafts, *L2* girth, *M* breeching/breech band, *N* crupper with no dockpiece, *O* loin strap and hip strap, *P* saddle, *Q* bridge, *R* harness bells (decorative), *S* housen, *T* hames, *U* hame strap, *V* neck strap, near side only (decorative), *W* 'fly' head terret – swinging disc in a hoop to repel flies (decorative), *X* rein hanger and hanging piece (decorative).

Trade sections

Trade turnout classes are specially for commercial vehicles, and they are sometimes subdivided into heavy and light trade sections. The former are devoted almost exclusively to Shires, Clydesdales, Percherons, Suffolk Punches or horses of the other heavy draught breeds and they are shown in either agricultural vehicles like farm wagons or heavy trade vehicles such as drays, while the light trade section covers all the other types including butchers' boxcarts, and milk floats. Horses with plenty of action are favoured for light trade classes and most are Hackney, Welsh Cob or a cross between the two. The whip should be dressed according to the trade his turnout represents, although in most cases a white coat over a suit and a bowler or straw hat is quite acceptable. Butchers and fishmongers both wear blue-and-white-striped aprons – horizontal stripes for a butcher, vertical stripes for a fishmonger. Sometimes a wooden bucket and nosebag are carried on a four-wheeled vehicle, slung from the rear axle. A few shows stage special classes for costermongers' turnouts, and these are especially popular with the spectators. The typical coster trolleys or spinners are loaded with a carefully packed display of fruit and flowers and the whole turnout is as colourful and eye-catching as possible. The schedule for such a class might read:

> BEST AND NEATEST COSTER'S TURNOUT. Ponies or donkeys. (Street traders.) Not more than two adults will be admitted with each vehicle. The judges will take into consideration the fact that the exhibits are properly kept and produced, having regard to their particular trade, and the manner in which they are presented, decorated and turned-out. Articles of ware must be carried on the vehicle.

Fine harness classes

In America, in addition to private or pleasure driving classes, fine harness classes, in which the quality and performance of the animal is paramount, are very popular. The horses are driven to very light four-wheeled fine harness buggies not unlike the show wagons and viceroys in which Hackney horses and ponies are shown. In American roadster classes the performance of the horse is again the main priority. The drivers wear 'silks' like racing jockeys and the horses are harnessed to very light sulky-type vehicles called bikes. The horses are shown at a jog trot, a faster trot called a road gait, and finally at a full-speed trot. Park classes are usually reserved for Morgan horses and these are for formal turnouts such as may have been used for park driving in the old days.

Coaching classes

Coaching classes are now confined to a handful of large shows, and cover three divisions: road or stage coaches which formerly carried fare-paying

DRESSAGE TEST

The Scale of Marks is as follows:-

10.	Excellent	5.	Sufficient
9.	Very good	4.	Insufficient
8.	Good	3.	Fairly bad
7.	Fairly Good	2.	Bad
6.	Satisfactory	1.	Very bad
		0.	Not performed

Competitor's No. .36..

TIME: 5 MINUTES

MOVEMENT			TO BE JUDGED	MARK 0-10	REMARKS
1.	A X	Enter at working trot Halt. Salute	Driving in on straight line Standing on the bit, transition	7	NICE ENTRY. HALT NOT QUITE SQUARE
2.	XCMB	Working trot	Transition, regularity, impulsion	7	NICE AND ACTIVE.
3.	B	Collected trot Circle right 20 metres	Regularity, impulsion, position and accuracy of figure	6	DIED A BIT IN FIRST PART OF CIRCLE. LOST IMPULSION.
4.	BFAK	Collected trot	Regularity, impulsion	7	POOR COLLECTION BUT GOOD FIGURE.
5.	KXM	Extended trot	Transition, regularity, impulsion	8	GOOD EXTENSION AND TRANSITIONS.
6.	MCHE	Collected trot	Transition, regularity, impulsion	7	SHOULD BE MORE DISTINCTION BETWEEN PACES.
7.	E	Collected trot, circle left 20 metres	Regularity, impulsion, position and accuracy of figure	5	HORSE EVADING BIT AND NOT GOING FORWARD.
8.	EKAD	Working trot	Regularity, impulsion	6	TOO SLOW
9.	DX	Walk	Transition, regularity, straightness	7	GOOD.
10.	X	Halt, immobility 10 seconds. Rein back 3 metres	Immobility, straightness	7	GOOD HALT. REIN-BACK NOT QUITE STRAIGHT
11.	XG G	Walk Halt. Salute Leave arena at working trot	Transitions, regularity straightness, standing on the bit	7	REGULAR BUT LACKING IMPULSION.
12.		Paces	-	6	INSUFFICIENT COLLECTION
13.		Impulsion	-	7	LACKING AT TIMES
14.		Obedience	-	7	OCCASIONAL RESISTANCE
15.		Driver	-	8	GOOD
			TOTAL:	102	

PRESENTATION: Rule 32
(if applicable)   (Max. + 10)   JUDGES SIGNATURE. A.N. Other.....

Figure 23 Example of a marked dressage test.

passengers, private coaches or 'drags', and regimental coaches. Road coaches are brightly painted with the names of the destinations emblazoned on the sides, and are heavier than drags, carrying fourteen roof passengers as opposed to twelve on a drag. The only 'groom' on a road coach is the guard, who should be appropriately dressed. Drags are sombrely painted, usually in the owner's family colours, although a discreet monogram or crest is permissible, and the two grooms wear matching livery. A regimental coach is similar to a drag but painted in the regimental colours with a regimental crest, and the grooms dress in livery with military cockades and regimental buttons. Although matching teams are usually preferred, a mixed team is acceptable with a road coach, as in coaching days it was common practice to have a grey or piebald leader which could be easily seen in the dark.

Concours d'élégance

In recent years *concours d'élégance* classes have become very popular with both competitors and spectators. Normal judging criteria do not apply, as these classes are judged by an artist who picks out those turnouts which in his or her eyes are the most elegant. Judging is done from a distance and turnouts are not closely inspected as in other show classes. The essence of *concours* classes is the word 'elegance', and the vehicle, horse, driver and passengers will all be taken into account, although it is the general impression more than anything which will count. Fancy dress or period costume is invariably barred. The performance of the horse(s) is not considered except that an unruly or disobedient horse may render an exhibit inelegant.

Combined driving

Combined driving was first practised on the Continent and introduced into Great Britain by HRH The Duke of Edinburgh. As the fastest-growing equestrian sport, it soon spread to America and Australia, where it enjoys increasing popularity too. In 1969 the Federation Equeste Internationale (generally abbreviated to FEI) drew up a set of rules and regulations for the organization and planning of international driving competitions. The first European Driving Championship was held at Budapest in 1971 when sixteen four-in-hand teams representing seven different countries took part. Four years later the rules were reviewed and a new edition of the rule book published. A full combined driving event consists of three quite separate phases: dressage, including presentation, a cross-country marathon, and obstacle cones, and the individual scores are collated to give an overall result. The presentation phase is to judge the turnout, cleanliness and general condition of horses, harness and vehicle as well as the position and dress of the driver and the attire and performance of the groom(s). Presentation is usually judged at the halt prior to the dressage test, but at some smaller events presentation may be judged 'on the move' while the competitor is performing his or her dressage test, and in such cases marks are awarded for general impression only. The object of the dressage test is to judge the freedom, regularity and distinction of paces, harmony, impulsion, suppleness and obedience of the horse(s) on the move. The test must be driven from memory in a measured arena and the competitor will be assessed on his or her style, accuracy and general command of the horses.

Calculation of penalty points for dressage

Maximum marks obtainable	**150**
Less average marks achieved (i.e. total marks divided by number of judges)	**102**
Penalty Points	**48**

Add: (to be marked on the President of the Jury's judging sheet only)

a. for errors of course and dismounting of grooms

First incident	5 penalty points
Second incident	10 penalty points
Third incident	15 penalty points
Fourth incident	Elimination
	Total —

b. Exceeding the time allowed
(0.5 penalty points per commenced second)

Time taken for test	seconds
Time allowed	300 seconds
Time exceeding time allowed	seconds
Penalty points (Time exceeding time allowed x 0.5 seconds)	

Total penalty points	**48**
Placing	—

Signature of President of Jury

Figure 24 Calculation of penalty points for dressage

The actual dressage test consists of a prescribed number of movements involving changes of pace and direction, and marks ranging from 0 to 10 are awarded for each movement as well as for paces, impulsion, obedience and driver. The total marks awarded by each judge are added together and divided by the number of judges, usually two, then deducted from the maximum possible to give a penalty score. The competitor with the lowest number of penalty marks will be highest placed in the dressage phase. It is always helpful when learning a test prior to an event to draw each movement on a piece of paper marked out with the letters of the arena. Practising the test too often with the horse and vehicle is not always such a good idea as a wily horse will soon begin to remember pars of the test and anticipate the movements, spoiling the overall effect. The paces required in a dressage test are as follows:

Walk: A regular four-beat rhythm, moving freely forward and covering the ground, the horse maintaining a light even contact with the reins.

Working trot: An active, well-balanced two-beat rhythm with the head carried more elevated than at the walk.

Collected trot: A shorter-striding, more animated pace without loss of impulsion or cadence with the head carried higher and the neck showing more flexion at the poll.

Extended trot: The hind legs well engaged to propel the horse forward with longer strides and less collection.

Reinback: Although not classed as a pace as such, the reinback is a two-beat rhythm and it should be straight, even and unrushed.

The cross-country marathon is to test the fitness and stamina of the horse and the skill and horsemanship of the competitor. The course is usually divided into five sections, the second and fourth sections being at a walk and the other three at a trot. A 'time allowed' is calculated for each section and penalties are assessed for exceeding this and for finishing a section before the minimum time. Penalties are also accrued for breaking from the specified pace for a section and for halts other than for an accident or hold-up on the course. Natural hazards like steep gradients are included in all but the walk sections, and in section C there are a number of artificial hazards to be negotiated. A penalty area extending twenty metres in all directions is marked out with a line of sawdust and the route(s) to be taken through the hazard marked out with red and white flags through which the competitor must drive. Penalties are assessed not only for exceeding the time allowed, but for grooms or passengers dismounting, the driver putting down his whip, disconnecting the traces, or turning over the vehicle, or for any part of the turnout leaving the penalty area before completing the hazard. The total penalties for the marathon are again calculated to determine the placings for that section of the event.

The last section of a combined driving event is the obstacle driving, in which the competitor must drive a course of about twenty pairs of obstacle cones within a time allowed, penalties being incurred for knocking over or displacing the obstacles, exceeding the time allowed, putting a groom down, error of course and so forth. Multiple obstacles may be included to make the course more interesting for competitors and spectators alike. Obstacles made up of elements of show jumps, straw bales or poles, and one water obstacle and/or one wooden bridge may also be used. Obstacle driving competitions can be judged by either of two methods: a 'fault competition' in which penalty points are accrued for displacing obstacles and exceeding the time allowed, or a 'time competition' in which penalty points are counted as seconds and added to the competitor's time for the course, the fastest time winning. The aim of this final section of the event is to test the fitness, obedience and suppleness of the horses after the marathon and the competence of the driver at precision driving. As in all comparatively new sports, the rules are constantly being reassessed and revised in the light of experience and as the sport develops, and at many small unaffiliated events the rules are modified to suit the circumstances.

Others

Still in the realm of competitive driving although quite different, the revival of interest in heavy horses has given the age-old traditions of ploughing a fillip and ensured the survival of skills that might otherwise have been lost. Ploughing matches are now an integral part of the British heavy horse scene and a National Ploughing Championship is held annually. In America, heavy draught competitions, which are essentially a test of strength, have become very popular in recent years.

Chapter 12
New technology

Horsepower as a serious means of transport is now virtually extinct, although the horse-drawn tourist carriage which can now be seen in most capital cities and resorts offering sightseeing tours has come to symbolize our more affluent and travel-conscious times. Many of these vehicles, including the fitton gharries of Bombay and the droitskas of Moscow, both of which resemble victorias, will have started life long ago as private carriages and fallen into the hands of cabmen only when they were no longer wanted, but other types of vehicles, notably the Irish jaunting car and the Canadian calèche, were built for passenger transport and easily made the transition to the tourist age. The horse trams of the Isle of Man are a big attraction for holidaymakers, and the Channel Island of Sark where motorized transport is banned has become the last bastion of commercial horse transport and holidaymakers flock to enjoy it.

The revival was centred on driving for pleasure, although it is highly probable that without competitive driving the sport would never have caught on and gained international momentum in the way it has. In the early years of renewed interest the only vehicles available were original traps and carriages, which were surprisingly numerous and correspondingly priced as the demand for them was still limited. Farm and large country-house sales, horse fairs and dealers' yards invariably produced a trap or two, and prospective purchasers were able to be discerning in their choice, more so as the cost of even minor repairs could come to more than the actual cost of the vehicle. Early driving rallies were unique in that virtually all the vehicles taking part were original, as at that time very few new ones were being built. As enthusiasm for the rediscovered sport of driving increased, the situation changed; the supply of original vehicles began to run out, pushing prices up and forcing people to look farther afield for vehicles. The Irish horse dealers were quick to begin collecting up any traps they could find and exporting them in large numbers to England, where regular carriages sales were now being held, as well as to America. The insatiable demand encouraged unscrupulous dealers to patch up unsound vehicles to make them saleable. Rotten wood could be filled with putty and painted over, cracked shafts inadequately repaired with metal plates or even glue, and worn rubbers were sometimes replaced with strips of car tyre nailed through the channel into the felloe. As buyers became aware of these practices and the dearth of good vehicles increased, there was a demand for new ones, and in due course the first modern vehicles were produced. These resembled traditional vehicles as closely as possible in design, the type of materials used and their method of construction, and they were used for pleasure driving, rallies and shows.

The introduction of rigorous new driving competitions such as combined and scurry driving created a need for particular types of vehicles, for, just as no one would enter a vintage car in a stock-car race, these new sports required specialized equipment. For the first time, the use of alternative materials had to be seriously considered, along with the possibility of new and better designs for the vehicles themselves. Significantly, the designs of the nineteenth-century coach builders could not be greatly improved upon, although for cross-country driving the decorative bodywork could be stripped away to shed weight, leaving only a skeleton body. Springs could be strengthened for driving over rough terrain with the addition of extra leaves or by supplementing their action with shock absorbers. Another new type of springing, the indispension unit, was also successfully tried out and found to reduce weight and give a smooth ride, albeit at the expense of appearances, for traditional springing looks far better. On particularly rough going it was found that by wrapping the springs with strong tape or even rope or by fitting the vehicle with spring 'stops' the risk of breakages could be reduced.

Metal wheels are often thought to be a recent innovation, but in fact back in 1894 the Bristol Wagon and Carriage Works Company had advertised 'cart and wagon wheels made entirely of iron', and added that 'many hundreds of pairs have been sent to India, North and South America, Africa and other tropical climates and the demand is constantly increasing'. Metal wheels are stronger in many respects than their wooden counterparts, but they lack the slight 'give' and flexibility of wood, although many early mishaps with metal wheels were caused by defects in their manufacture, as the building of wheels, whether of wood or metal, is a highly skilled job. The coach builders of the early nineteenth century had been indefatigable experimenters and had, over a period of time, tested a number of innovations with regard to the manufacture of carriage wheels, few of which proved to be of any real worth. Once it was ascertained that elasticity in a wheel rendered it less likely to suffer damage from constant concussion, various innovations were put to the test. William Bridges Adams, in *English Pleasure Carriages*, 1837, expressed a belief that an 'elastic wheel acting in all directions would be a great and obvious improvement' and the dished wheel was soon found to incorporate the necessary qualities of flexibility and strength. Dished wheels, which are shaped in such a way that the spokes slope outwards from the hub to the felloe, are fitted to an axle tree which is also shaped so that the spokes below the hub remain vertical while the spokes above the hub slope outwards. In addition to increased strength, a dished wheel imposes less strain on the axle nuts and the danger of the wheel coming off is greatly reduced. As the distance between the top of the wheel and the vehicle body is increased without altering the track width on the ground, less dirt is thrown up by the wheels on to the vehicle and passengers. The spokes are generally staggered where they fit into the hub, or secured by a metal collar called a warner band which fits tightly around the hub. Less successful inventions included wheels with leather spokes, which 'lacked firmness to say nothing of want of durability' (*English Pleasure Carriages*) , and wheels with spiral springs instead of rigid spokes, which were quite useless. Other ideas for incorporating steel springs in the actual wheel also proved impracticable on account of cost, additional weight, breaking springs or unacceptable rattling, and most looked unsightly.

When very light elegant carriages became fashionable, wheel hubs or naves of a large diameter were felt to be excessive in relation to the rest of the vehicle and the coach builders sought a way to reduce the size and weight of the hub without sacrificing strength. In 1805 Samuel Miller patented his method of building wheels with no proper hub at all. Instead the nave ends of the spokes were tapered in a radial direction so that they fitted side by side around the axlebox. The spokes were secured by two metal discs which were actually integral parts of the box casting, and the spokes were driven so tightly together in the groove between the discs that they were prevented from rotating around the box. The tapered spoke roots in wheels of this type led to the term 'wedge wheel' by which they were known, although they were so extensively used by the army that the name 'artillery wheel' is now more common. The adventurous new coach builders of recent years have tried metal wheels with shaped oval spokes and aluminium hubs and have experimented with various alloys, with mixed results. An epoxy resin hub has also been used with some success, and roller bearings have become standard on all metal hubs.

Traditionally, hand brakes with a simple ratchet were fitted to most four-wheeled vehicles, although screw-on brakes were also fitted on some Continental vehicles and a few had foot brakes which operated a wooden block on the tyre. For cross-country driving a brake is necessary, and one or two enterprising people tried fitting disc brakes to original vehicles with wooden wheels. It was not a success, as when applied at speed the brake was so severe that it weakened the spokes or even caused the wheel to disintegrate. On metal wheels, however, disc and drum brakes work well. Old-fashioned wood block brakes work best on iron tyres, as they can cause rubber tyres to slacken or even come out of the channel.

More recently fibreglass has been used in the manufacture of vehicle bodies, as well as for shafts, as it combines lightness with strength and fibreglass shafts have considerable spring in them. The lack of traditional materials for the making of carriage parts has often led to the discovery of substitutes which have proved excellent for the purpose, and when modern coach builders could not get supplies of lancewood for shafts they tried a revolutionary new idea. By glueing together layers of ash, a laminated shaft with the elastic qualities of lancewood was produced, which could be steam-bent without losing any of its inherent strength. Lancewood could be only slightly bent. Various types of plastics have also been tested with the manufacture of shafts in mind, although none has as yet proved to be of any particular merit. Purists may regard these innovations with scepticism, just as the Victorians sneered with disapproval at the first use of plywood for vehicle bodies, but their use has helped to update the sport of driving by combining old traditions with new technology.

In recent years a series of new designs for competition vehicles has been produced, with the emphasis on strength and practicality rather than aesthetic value, and these more than anything reflect the use of modern technology to meet the demands of a discerning and specialist market. Many of these functional vehicles are built with a metal frame faced with plywood panels, complete with false louvres to give the appearance of a traditional dogcart, while others in the two-wheeled range consist of little more than a seat, wheels, springs and shafts, the object being to keep overall weight to a minimum. Tubular metal shafts which can be shaped to look like double-bend wooden shafts are standard on many, as are steel poles, some with springs built into the housing on the forecarriage, on many four-wheeled vehicles on which a broken pole could mean possible elimination from a cross-country event. Telescopic axles which can be adjusted to suit different types of competitions are typical of features relevant to vehicles used solely for competitive events. The track width can be reduced or increased by simply jacking up the vehicle and removing the securing pins to release the axle extensions, which carry the wheels and which slide in and out of the tubular axle. Adaptable seating arrangements which can be altered to suit different purposes are another feature of dual-purpose vehicles, and more recently, examples on which the panels can be unbolted to lighten and streamline the vehicle for cross-country work have been produced. Heavy-duty springs, shock absorbers and indispension units provide the suspension, and the purpose-built steel wheels are protected from being caught on trees or gateposts by reinforced mudguards which project over the wheels to form a type of safety bar. While standardizing competition vehicles by imposing minimum weights, track widths and other criteria may help to give competitors in combined driving events fewer advantages over each other, it is likely that the increased financial expenditure necessary to purchase such equipment will tend to make the sport exclusive. Many original American and Australian vehicles were designed to be used on rough tracks and dirt roads and have been successfully used for modern competitive events with few adaptations, the Meadowbrook being a perfect example.

One of the most revolutionary designs of vehicle to come out must be the equirotal phaeton which is built in two quite separate sections, held together by a central kingpin which allows the front and rear halves to flex like an articulated vehicle. Its makers claim that it is more manoeuvrable and therefore easier to drive through tight hazards in competitions, although not everyone who has driven one subscribes to this view. Its other claim to fame rests in the fact that when turning sharply the boxseat turns with the whole front section so that the driver is always facing in the same direction as his horses, as he would be when driving a single horse to a two-wheeled vehicle. One of the many disadvantages is that an equirotal phaeton is difficult to reverse. The idea of articulated vehicles is not new; the inventor and engineer William Bridges Adams first thought of such vehicles back in the 1830s. He built many types of carriages using his basic pattern of a central hinge and four wheels of equal size, and worked tirelessly to interest the general public in his invention. Equirotal phaetons, town chariots, omnibuses and even a coach were built under the auspices of the inventor's brother, who was a sleeping partner in the coach-building firm of Hobson and Co. of Long Acre, London where, it was advertised, 'equirotal carriages for private use are manufactured in the best manner, and where orders, personally or by letter, will be promptly attended to'.

Not all new vehicles are designed with rough treatment on cross-country marathons in mind, as private driving and *concours d'élégance* classes are very popular and these require show vehicles built and finished to a high standard. In stark contrast to the many new designs and inventions applied to what are generally termed 'competition vehicles', show vehicles are based almost exclusively on original designs. Two- and four-wheeled dogcarts, phaetons, gigs and ralli cars predominate in show classes, and modern carriage builders can turn out vehicles of such a high quality that only the most discerning would be able to tell them from a professionally restored original. Stylish curved bodies can be achieved by the use of laminated wood with a steel chassis to give added strength, and woven cane panels are sometimes used to suggest lightness and elegance.

Harness makers kept abreast with progress by experimenting with new types of materials which would serve the same purpose as leather and yet be less expensive and easier to maintain. Harness made with poor-quality leather, much of it imported from abroad, proved unsatisfactory as the material was weak and liable to break under strain, and the standard of the craftsmanship left much to be desired. Leather substitutes including cotton webbing, nylon and 'buffalo hide' proved quite successful, although other materials including plastics lacked the necessary strength, tended to stretch and could also rub the horse, particularly if it was sweated up. The new types of harness were generally lighter in weight and could easily be cleaned by washing in hot soapy water. Although good-quality leather harness is unlikely to be seriously rivalled by these recent introductions, the new alternatives have much to recommend them.

Anyone contemplating building their own vehicle should weigh up the pros and cons objectively before embarking on the project, as in many cases little, if anything, will be saved financially and the involvement in terms of time can be quite considerable. Many modern coach builders, particularly those who specialize in the manufacture of metal competition or exercise vehicles, can produce them under factory-line conditions, unlike the old coach builders who built each carriage to order, and although the basic and well-tested design may be amended slightly to suit specific requirements, mass production methods, including bulk buying, can greatly reduce the cost. The replacement of parts, which can be a major consideration if the vehicle is to be used for cross-country competitions, can generally be done from stock, and at least one large manufacturer can supply wheels of varying sizes which fit the standard stub axle to make the vehicle suit different sizes of horses, the shafts being adjustable for length and, on some models, width as well.

Wheels and axles are the most expensive individual items to be purchased, and the range of suppliers, most of whom advertise in the driving magazines and society publications, is quite extensive. The size of the wheel will depend upon the size of the horse or pony for whom the vehicle is being built, but for a pony of 13.2 – 14 hh. the wheel should not exceed 48 in. and should be not less than 42 in. The choice of wood or metal construction will be dictated by personal preference and available funds, wooden wheels being more costly, but rubber tyres are preferable to metal hoops which are very noisy on roads or stony tracks. Rubber tyres do not wear for as long and in very heavy mud can pull out of the channel, but renewing rubber tyres is not a big job and a loose tyre can be replaced at home by tapping it carefully into the channel with a blunt chisel and hammer. Buying wheels without axles is always a gamble, as it may prove very expensive or nearly impossible to find an axle to fit them. Many new wheels fit a standard 1-in. stub axle. Loose spokes can sometimes be rectified by soaking the wheel in water to swell the wood, but if this does not work an expensive visit to the wheelwright may be called for. At sales, always check that the wheels are a true pair, sound and not unequally dished as a result of the tyre being put on one too tightly. Spinning the wheel on the axle will show up warped or buckled wheels.

The form of springing used must be appropriate to the style of vehicle and the use to which it will be put. The design of the vehicle may preclude the use of some types of suspension, and the estimated weight of the loaded body will dictate the size and width of the springs, the number of leaves in each spring, and whether shackles are used to increase the movement. A vehicle with over-soft springing can be just as uncomfortable and tiring as one which is very hard-sprung. On some vehicles the shafts are attached to a spring leaf at the rear of the vehicle and a pivot at the front, and this improves the way the vehicle rides. Trace hooks which are bolted to a very short leaf spring through the splinter bar at the front of the vehicle reduce the risk of the horse getting sore shoulders, particularly if driven in a breast collar, as they work in the same way as a swingletree.

Wooden shafts look better than metal shafts but are more expensive to buy or replace should one get broken, in view of the time and skill required to make them. Metal shafts are not expensive to produce and can be bent to almost any shape with comparative ease. In the event of a serious accident a wooden shaft will break, whereas a metal shaft will only bend; this can hold drawbacks as well as advantages. Curved shafts allow a larger horse to be put to the vehicle without having to raise the height of the body, and 'double sweep' shafts also curve in towards the horse's shoulders to fit closer while leaving plenty of room for the horse's hindquarters. Shafts are best attached to the outside of the vehicle, as integral shafts which enter the vehicle through holes in the footboard and run along the inside on the floor tend to produce a vibrating effect if the vehicle is not perfectly balanced.

The design of the body should be compatible with the type of horse as well as to the function of the completed vehicle. Many amateur coach builders will wish to produce a general-purpose vehicle capable of fulfilling a number of roles – smart enough to show, yet robust enough to take on rally drives or even cross-country marathons. Features like spindled seats enhance the appearance, but metal spindles will not splinter on rough tracks as wooden ones tend to. On the other hand, a solid round-backed seat is warmer in cold or windy weather. A few visits to museum collections or shows where driving classes are held, armed with a tape-measure, pencil and paper, should provide plenty of ideas, and the actual measurement of the seat in relation to the floor and dashboard can be made to suit the height of the driver. Nothing is worse than being unable to reach the footboard, or being cramped in a tiny vehicle, knees under chin, because there is insufficient leg room. The framework of the body needs to be very strong, as it is subjected to severe stress from different angles when turning or driving over rough ground.

The greatest problem will most likely be ensuring that the vehicle, if it is two-wheeled, balances correctly. If the vehicle is either too low or too high, or if when loaded there is too much or too little weight on the shafts, the vehicle will be unbalanced. The height of a vehicle can be altered a few inches by placing or removing wooden blocks between the springs and the flat plate on the axle to which they are bolted. Vehicles with a sliding seat can easily be balanced by moving the seat backwards, if the vehicle is 'heavy on', or forwards if it is 'light on'. A winding handle or simple ratchet device is usually employed to move the seat. Gigs or two-wheeled vehicles with an immovable seat must be carefully designed to balance properly with the seat right over the axle. Slight adjustments can be made by moving the axle a little way up or down the springs, or by raising or lowering the shaft tugs on the harness.

Lamp brackets are best sited between the wheel and the body, provided there is plenty of room for the lamps, which take up more space than might be imagined. There must be adequate clearance below the mudguards to get the lamps in and out, and they should not be so close to the wheels that they are likely to touch should the vehicle bottom on its springs on very rough terrain. Lamp brackets on the dashboard should be avoided, as they are liable to be caught by the reins and are also vulnerable to damage from the horse, should it kick. The whip holder should be fixed to the offside of the body within easy reach of the driver. A whip holder on the dashboard is wrong, since when the whip is in the holder it will get in the way of the reins when mounting the vehicle.

For anyone wishing to put together a turnout there are several alternative ways of doing so, beginning with the sale ring. Regular sales, not only of vehicles but harness, carriage parts and driving accoutrements, are held regularly on both sides of the Atlantic and bargains may be picked up if you are prepared to take a gamble. Should a vehicle be bought which on close inspection at home proves to be unsuitable, there is no way of returning or exchanging it, and it is easy in the tense atmosphere of an auction to bid higher than you had really intended to. However, sales do offer a wide selection of vehicles all in one place, so that comparisons may be made. If buying at sales, it is advisable to go prepared with comprehensive measurements of what you require, and to check over any possible purchases meticulously before bidding for them in the sale ring, to no more than a price limit decided beforehand. Sales are not an indication of market values, as it needs only two people bidding at one lot to inflate the price out of all proportion. Vehicles requiring restoration may prove to be more expensive than those in show condition in the long run, when the cost of restoration has been added to the purchase price, and sometimes the real bargains are in the upper end of the price range. The important measurements to take to a sale are the shaft height at the tug stops when the vehicle is held with the floor horizontal, and the width of the shafts at the tugstops and dashboard. For harness, the inside measurement of the collar is essential and the girth circumference may be helpful.

The decision of whether to purchase a new or original vehicle needs to be carefully considered. The proliferation of new coach builders has widened the choice of vehicles on the market and caused prices generally to level out, although outstanding original vehicles still command high prices and tend to maintain their value. However, the uses to which an antique vehicle can be put will be limited by its age, value and suitability for the purpose, whereas a new vehicle may be less expensive and more adaptable, although it will not appreciate in value at the same rate as an original. The choice and availability of new vehicles and the warranties and after-sales service which many manufacturers offer need to be taken into account as well. Buying privately from vendors who advertise in the equestrian or driving press or in club newsletters can involve many miles of travelling to look at vehicles which may be quite unsuitable. Coach builder's illustrated brochures giving full details of their vehicles, including the price, will give some indication of what is available within your price range, and a visit to the factory or showroom to inspect the vehicles may convince you of the wisdom or otherwise of your choice. Recently, vehicles in kit form which can be assembled at home have come on the market, helping to reduce the cost of new vehicles even further and bringing driving more and more within the reach of ordinary people.

Chapter 13
Miscellany

It is surprising to note how many of the expressions we use in everyday language owe their origins to the days of coaching and horse-drawn transport. Some sayings, like 'kicking over the traces', would be virtually self-explanatory to a generation whose day-to-day travel relied so much on the horse, but with other expressions the true meaning have become obscured by time, and their significance would elude most present-day motorists.

A lively person is often said to be 'full of beans', and this saying dates back to the last century and the jobmasters who hired out hansom cabs and horses on a daily basis to cabmen who did not possess turnouts of their own. Long hours of hard work were necessary if the cabman was to recover the hiring fee and make a profit for himself, and a fit and keen horse was a great help. In return for a tip, the jobmaster's ostler would see that the horse was given extra rations of beans, which were very heating and certain to make the horse lively. It would prance out of the jobmaster's yard in the morning truly 'full of beans'. Ostlers were responsible for the health and soundness of the horses they cared for, and a sick horse was an unprofitable one. From the ostlers we get the term 'getting back into harness' which we use to mean returning to work after sickness or a holiday.

The Americans have a saying, 'putting a mule in horse's harness', which might baffle people now for an original meaning, but which would have seemed logical at a time when people were familiar with the characteristics of both animals, including the stubborn nature of the mule.

An important person who coordinates or holds together an organization or specific situation is often referred to as the 'kingpin', but the kingpin is literally the bolt which attaches the forecarriage to the rest of a four-wheeled vehicle and is therefore of vital importance. The phrase 'to put your shoulder to the wheel' is a reminder of coaching days and the rutted, pot-holed roads at the time. Passengers not infrequently had to get out of the vehicle and literally put their shoulders to the wheel to free the coach so that they could continue on their journey. Another coaching expression is 'rank outsider', which at one time referred to the passenger who had the seat next to the guard on the back of a coach.

The common expression 'to drop off to sleep' is thought to come from the days when passengers travelled on the roof of a road coach for a reduced fare, and not infrequently fell asleep and 'dropped off', with fatal results. 'As right as the mails' referred to the times when the mail coaches were so punctual that people set their pocket watches by them, and 'post haste', meaning 'without delay', comes from the postboys who at one time provided a speedy if expensive mail or passenger service between towns. 'Milestones' were the roadside markers which mail guards used to calculate the speed at which the coach was travelling, and an 'old stager' was a horse which had worked many 'stages', or stretches of road between inns.

'Raring to go' was originally 'rearing to go', as apparently was sometimes the case with fit, corned-up horses in city traffic jams. 'Headstrong' denoted a horse that was hard-mouthed and difficult to hold, and the word 'curb' is still used to mean restraint in a number of contexts without allusion to horses or bits. The word 'stumer', meaning a failure, was at one time a north-country word for a useless horse, and the term 'slacker' for a lazy person really referred to the lazy horse in a pair, whose traces were always slack. The other horse, who did the bulk of the work, was said to 'set the pace' – a term we still use for someone who sets a standard. In Britain, taxis are still licensed as 'hackney carriages' but referred to as 'cabs' by the general public on both sides of the Atlantic, and engine capacities are assessed in terms of horse power, but it is not just old expressions which belie our horse-powered roots.

It is customary for the driver of a horse-drawn vehicle to sit on the offside. This custom was well established long before any codes of practice for road users were introduced. In all methods of holding the reins for driving, the whip is held in the right hand, and by sitting on the offside of the vehicle the right arm is not restricted by the close proximity of a passenger when using the whip. If the driver sat on the nearside of the vehicle, the passenger would be constantly nudged in the ribs by the driver's right elbow, and the chances of the unfortunate passenger being struck in the face by the whip thong would be greatly increased. The ability to place a whip exactly where required, then catch the thong on the stick again afterwards, was a highly esteemed skill, and coachmen prided themselves on being able to touch the nearside leader in a team with the thong without startling or upsetting the other three horses. It is said that many of the old coachmen were so adept with a whip that they could knock a fly off a horse without the horse even being aware of what was happening. Street urchins who sneaked rides on the back springs of town carriages learned to leap off quickly when 'whip behind' was called from the pavement, and the coachman's whip was laid across the roof to strike the unwelcome passengers and cause them to lose their precarious hold.

Such expressions and traditions may be the legacy of a horse-powered era, but little evidence is left of some of the less-than-successful inventions which have been tried out in a vain attempt to revolutionize the horse-drawn vehicle. The Roman Emperor Commodus, who was murdered in AD 192, had in his collection of vehicles a 'horseless carriage' which housed in its structure a number of slaves who drove the vehicle with their hands and feet. Another of his ingenious vehicles had a mileometer which dropped a small stone into a metal cup after each mile, thereby indicating the distance travelled.

Another short-lived experiment was an immense vehicle driven by a large draught horse on a giant treadmill inside the vehicle, while in England a much smaller vehicle on rails but driven by a horse on a movable belt was experimented with. A vehicle attached to the side of the horse like a motorbike side-car was suggested; there was a three-wheeled hansom cab and a governess car with a side door, and in France there was a curious vehicle called an 'equibus', which resembled an enclosed jaunting car seating four people plus the driver on the front. It had no shafts, as the vehicle was built in an arch to go over the horse's back, the wheels being attached to the underside on either stub axles or an arch-shaped axle. The noted painter, James Pollard, was responsible for a painting entitled *Mr Sharp's Tandem*, which shows the shafts of the vehicle as curved and joined at the front to encircle the wheeler's chest, the leader's traces being attached to a swingletree hooked on to a 'crab' on the joined shafts. It is highly probable that the Mr Sharp in the painting was James Sharp, an engineer, designer and builder of 'exceptionally original' agricultural carts with rollers instead of wheels, in which case he probably designed the shafts on his tandem cart.

Even horseless carriages had been invented by 1649 when Johann Hautsch, a Nuremberg mechanic, drove through the streets in a strange vehicle he had designed and constructed himself. It was driven by manually operated levers and cog-wheels and on flat ground could move along at a speed of 'two thousand steps an hour'. The ornate body resembled a phaeton but with lavish carving including a dragon's head at the front and trumpeting angels above the side panels. If curious spectators pressed too closely the trumpets sounded and the dragon spurted water while its eyes rolled. The Swedish crown prince, Charles Gustavus, bought the vehicle from Hautsch and used it in the coronation parade when he ascended the throne. Hautsch's design attracted interest from other quarters too and Stephen Farfler, a legless watchmaker who lived near Nuremberg, copied the design and built himself a three-wheeled vehicle driven by hand-operated handles attached to the front wheel.

A number of amateur whips, including Lord Astley, drove their horses with the very minimum of harness in order to be daring and different, but few were quite as brave as Charles Enderby, whose portrait, painted in 1837 by F.C. Turner, shows him driving his horse, Arterxerxes, in a Tilbury gig with no bridle, collar, traces or breeching. Instead, the shafts, which curve sharply where they go through the tugs, act as both traces and breeching, and the bit is held in the horse's mouth by pressure on the reins only.

The adventurous and inventive people responsible for these curious turnouts were very much a minority and their short-lived creations were generally assumed to be the outlandish whims of eccentrics. However, there have been many attempts to use animals other than horses or ponies in harness work, usually in serious bids to utilize available power, rather than as frivolous experiments. Donkeys and mules have been driven in harness since very early times, and in the Far East camels are a familiar sight, singly or in pairs, pulling all types of vehicles including water carts. Oxen are another traditional draught animal, since they are both strong and docile, and the Boers used them in large numbers in South Africa as they were well able to cope with the rugged terrain and heat and were immune to many of the diseases which plagued horses. Quite recently at a South African show a most unusual eight-in-hand turnout made an appearance, consisting of a pair of Hackney ponies in the lead, followed by a pair of mules, then a pair of donkeys and finally a pair of oxen.

A zebra is reputed to be one of the most difficult animals to break in and train, being vicious and obstinate, but Mr Leopold de Rothschild, a member of the wealthy banking family, drove a four-in-hand of them and was even photographed with his bizarre team outside the Albert Hall in London in 1896. They were regularly driven in Hyde Park, to the amazement of passers-by, although they had to be taken out early in the morning before the roads were busy as other horses were frightened of them. Genetically, the zebra is as close a relative to the donkey as to the horse, and attempts to cross the zebra with the horse have only resulted in a type of mule called a zebroid. These mules are unique as they are generally bay or brown with a limited number of black stripes on the body and legs, but they have shown themselves to be more reliable in harness than their striped forebears. A gentleman in Alaska succeeded in driving a team of llamas to a low two-wheeled sulky, having bought them when they were six months old and had them professionally broken to harness.

Dogs have been used for draught purposes since time immemorial, and husky teams are used to this day in the far north. On the Continent large dogs were used to pull little two-wheeled carts laden with dairy produce or vegetables from the small farms to the weekly markets, and the North American Indians used dogs to drag small slidecars when they moved camp. At one Irish country house they kept a tiny wicker governess car lined with leather and drawn by an Irish wolfhound, which gave children rides around the garden. The goat cart was the toy of wealthy Victorian children and many large houses kept one for use during the summer months. Very light in weight with wire wheels, fine springs and shafts, the goat cart could be drawn by either one or two goats which were harnessed to the vehicle with leather breast-collar harness.

There have been a few instances of sheep being trained to pull small vehicles and it is recorded that when Napoleon's son first began to walk he was given a tiny phaeton painted blue and slung on cee-springs. Drawn by a

pair of pet lambs, he rode around the terrace of the Tuileries in it. A man
from Suffolk trained a pig to pull a small cart on pneumatic tyres, and there
are many examples of different types of deer being used in harness. In South
Africa ostriches have been trained to pull very light chariot-type vehicles in
which they are raced as a means of entertainment, and there is even an
instance of a chicken being harnessed by means of a breast strap and girth to
a miniature four-wheeled cart in which a baby rode, armed with a whip!

Driving has produced some eccentric and colourful characters, from the
suicidal charioteers of ancient Rome to the 'red-faced inebriate cabmen' of
Dickensian England and the stage-coach drivers of the American Wild
West. Some, like the Hungarian Count Sandor, were exceptional horsemen
who used daring and dangerous feats to demonstrate their unique abilities.
The Count, who used to startle passers-by when out riding by jumping his
horse over moving carriages, maintained a large stable of fine harness
horses and regularly drove a four-in-hand through the streets of Budapest,
where he lived. His most famous exploit occurred in 1827, when he was out
driving in an open carriage accompanied by John Presstel, the German
artist, and a groom. A very steep flight of stone steps ran from the winding
street near the Count's mansion high above the city down to the River
Danube below, and Count Sandor was just about to pass the stairway when
he turned his team sharply and drove headlong down the stone steps.
Amazingly, the horses managed to keep their feet and hold back the
carriage, which somehow survived the violent rattling it received as the
wheels bounced from step to step.

John Mytton, the squire of Halston in Shropshire, was a madman with a
predilection for brandy, whose foolhardy feats in the early 1800s earned
him the name of Mad Mytton. On one occasion he drove a tandem across
country, over hedges and ditches in the dark for a bet of £25, and on
another occasion he was accompanied by an unsuspecting passenger who
confided in Mytton that he had never been tipped out of a gig. On hearing
this, Mytton ran one wheel up a bank and overturned the gig, tipping them
both out. He is best remembered for an incident when he was trying out two
horses in tandem and inquired of the vendor, a dealer who was sitting next
to him in the gig, if the leader could jump. Not being convinced by the
dealer's answer, he put the horses at a gate. The leader sailed over, leaving
the wheeler, the remains of the gig and the two men on the other side.

Lord Barrymore was another eccentric who, when driving home in his
phaeton after nights on the town, amused himself by breaking the darkened
windows of village houses by striking them with his whip as he hurtled past.
He euphemistically called it 'fanning the daylights', and the sound of
splintering glass would make him roar with laughter. The old coachman
who used to drive Lord Barrymore on his rounds of the London brothels two
or three times a week was quite a character himself. He recalled that, 'after
waiting till near daylight, or till daylight, I've carried my lord, girls and all
– fine, dressed-up madams – to Billingsgate, and there I've left them to

breakfast at some queer place, or to slang with fishwives. What times them was, to be sure!' (H. Mayhew, *London Labour and the London Poor*, 1861.)

Madame Pompadour, the fashion-conscious and beautiful mistress of Louis XV of France, was famous for her pale-blue and pink carriages, in which she drove through the woods near her château in the Dordogne, her extravagant dresses matching the colours of the carriages. One Indian maharajah maintained an even more garish turnout in which Lord Baden-Powell once rode. The elegant barouche was drawn by a pair of white horses whose tails had been dyed a brilliant pink to match the liveries of the driver and grooms.

Lord Lonsdale was an outstanding sportsman who kept a stable of high-quality chestnut horses and a coach house filled with yellow vehicles which earned him the nickname of the 'yellow Earl'. Already a notable horseman with a number of equestrian feats to his credit, he achieved world-wide fame in 1891 when he drove twenty miles in four five-mile laps, using four different equipages, in under an hour. The feat was originally to be a race between Lord Lonsdale and Lord Shrewsbury, but the latter withdrew at the last minute and Lord Lonsdale decided to run the match against time so as not to disappoint the large crowd that had assembled to watch. Using a single horse in an American buggy, a pair in a four-wheeled vehicle, a team in a brake, and a postillion pair in the buggy again, he finished the course in fifty-five and a half minutes.

Fortunately, as the carriage-driving eccentrics of one generation pass into history, another group takes their place, and the modern driving fraternity has as many members keen to drive more horses farther and faster than anyone else as any previous generation ever had.

Chapter 14
Future prospects

Speculating on the future of any sport or leisure activity is a precarious
occupation, for changing trends mean that today's sports may be outdated
tomorrow, and yesterday's pastimes poised for rediscovery. The prognosis
for all leisure sports is good, as a result of increased free time together with
better sports facilities and a proliferation of clubs and organizations to foster
individual sports regionally and nationally. To survive in the long run in
competition with other leisure pursuits, a sport needs to be adaptable and
progressive, and carriage driving embodies these qualities while remaining
firmly rooted in old traditions which give the sport a sound foundation and
a feeling of continuity which other sports may lack. Under the umbrella
title of carriage-driving, the many facets of the sport offer enormous scope
and choice to those interested in the harnessing of horse power for a diverse
range of activities, as well as unlimited potential to designers and engineers,
craftsmen and artisans eager to introduce new thinking to an age-old means
of transport.

Until very recently, the opportunities for those wishing to learn to drive
horses were few and far between. A hundred years ago young men were
often taught to drive by the family coachman, while others learnt their skills
in the army, as most countries maintained horse artillery and cavalry
regiments well into the twentieth century. Young workmen were shown the
basics of driving horses by the wagoners and foremen they worked under,
and for those who could afford to pay generous tips to unscrupulous
coachmen the mail coaches provided a rare opportunity to drive a four-in-
hand under the watchful eye of an expert. In the last few years a number of
establishments offering tuition in all aspects of carriage driving have been
opened, although they are still greatly outnumbered by riding schools and
many tend to be exclusive and expensive. The driving clubs and societies
also arrange instructional days and lectures for the benefit of their
members, but readily available competitively priced driving instruction is
still a thing of the future.

Driving has undoubtedly had an effect on the fortunes of many breeds of
horses and ponies by bringing into prominence again long-established
harness breeds which were in danger of being lost through cross-breeding to

produce horses of a better riding type. Many of the European pony breeds, particularly the smaller ones like the Shetland, were in peril of becoming ornamental rather than functional. Driving has given them an opportunity to prove their worth again as utility breeds, and it is probable that still other breeds have been saved from near-extinction by the sport. Critics will argue that the driving boom has been detrimental to some breeds by introducing foreign blood, usually Hackney, in an attempt to improve action and type at the expense of breed character. Progress without change is rarely achieved, and new types of crosses, often using breeds whose harness qualities have been forgotten, are constantly being tried with the aim of producing horses better suited to today's specialized market. It is possible that in future years a new harness breed will evolve as a result.

The future of the sport lies in competitive driving, which is now the fastest-growing equestrian sport in Britain, with a very keen following on the Continent and in the United States. Analysing why it should be so popular is difficult, as different aspects of the sport attract people for varying reasons. The excitement of harness racing in sulkies is indisputable, and draws huge crowds of spectators, especially in America. With perhaps the exception of scurry driving and chuck-wagon racing, which are also both speed events, most of the other forms of competitive driving do not fall within the category of spectator sports. Combined driving is a potential exception as it has much to offer spectators, being based on the ridden three-day event which enjoys capacity audiences at all the major venues. Although teams provide the greatest spectacle, the owners and drivers of single-horse or pony turnouts are the most numerous representatives of the sport, and although most national events make provision for single, pair and tandem turnouts as well as teams in their classification, the European and world championships are open to teams only. If singles, pairs and tandems could qualify for and compete at world championship level this would generate tremendous new interest among those who are competitively ambitious and see only limited scope for single turnouts. The argument that syndicate-owned teams can and have taken part in such events, thereby giving individuals who could not afford to keep a team of their own an opportunity to take part, is frequently put forward in defence of team-only events, but it does not justify the exclusion of single, pair and tandem competitors. Increased interest and higher entries at all events would attract bigger sponsors, and in view of the exorbitant cost of staging large events, it is difficult to see how the sport can develop successfully without the backing of sponsorship. Inevitably, substantial sponsorship would attract the interest of the press and media, and increased coverage would help to market the sport as a spectator event. Marathon courses would then have to be planned with spectators as well as competitors in mind. Hazards would have to be imaginative and interesting, and arranged on the course so that they were accessible to spectators, who should be able to watch from good vantage points. Having the hazards in small clusters would minimize the amount of walking competitors would need to do in order to see all hazards on the course.

On the basis that necessity is the mother of invention, new developments, not only in vehicles, but in harness and sundry equipment, will proliferate only if the demand remains consistent. The striving to produce better horse-drawn vehicles at more competitive prices has already had a dramatic effect on the types of vehicles in use and the number of people who can afford to buy and drive them. New designs incorporating revolutionary features are regularly put on the market at prices intended to undercut other manufacturers, and these introductions streamline the market, pushing up quality and value for money simultaneously. This system will be perpetuated as new technology and new designs are produced to adapt to changing demands, thereby ensuring that the sport does not become static. New materials, as yet undiscovered, may radically alter our concept of carriage construction in the same way as today's moulded fibreglass trap bodies would have seemed extraordinary to Victorian carriage builders, but it is important not to lose sight of the old traditions of which the sport is merely an updated continuation, rather than a highly technical offshoot.

When the revival first started to gain momentum in the early 1950s such activities as combined driving and scurry driving, to name but two, were unheard-of, and it is likely that future years will see new sports emerge under the banner of carriage driving. Standards in driving competitions rise every year as people's skill and experience increase, particularly as a result of combined driving, and cross-country courses which were regarded as difficult ten years ago would cause few problems for competitors now. By increasing the difficulty factor, standards improve, and so the range and severity of competitions will alter in years to come to match the ability of participants. Although by comparison fewer people drive horses today than a century ago, today's drivers are probably more skilled, as they push themselves further, experiment and take greater risks in order to increase their skills than their predecessors ever dared to do. At a time when an overturned carriage meant instant dismissal for a coachman with little hope of re-employment elsewhere, cautious driving was a necessity, and no coachman would have chanced doing some of the things which today's drivers regularly attempt when taking part in competitive events.

Optimism is a characteristic of speculators, but improving standards all round augur for a bright future for carriage driving, not only in Europe and the United States, but also in other countries where driving is still in its second infancy. Although the return of commercial horse-drawn transport is little more than a pipedream, the driving of horses for pleasure will undoubtedly survive, and present-day drivers are responsible for helping to carry forward for the benefit of generations to come the traditions and skills handed down from previous eras when the horse and carriage reigned supreme.

Glossary of technical terms

axle arm: the shaped end of the axle on which the wheel of the vehicle rotates. Sometimes called the axle tree.

axle bed: the centre part of the axle to which the axle arms are attached at either end.

axle box: the centre of the hub of the wheel into which the axle arm is fixed.

bars: coaching term for a set of swingletrees.

buggy: in America a general term for four-wheeled owner-driven vehicles. In Britain the term is sometimes used to describe a hooded gig.

box: raised seat from which a coach or carriage is driven.

chamfer: the shaving or planing of the spokes or framework of a vehicle to improve the appearance and reduce weight.

channel: the metal rim attaching the rubber tyre to the felloes of a wheel.

chassis: the metal or wooden underframe of a vehicle.

cock horse: a ridden horse hitched to the front of a team to provide additional power when ascending steep hills.

coupling rein: the short piece of a pair rein buckled on to the longer draught rein.

cutter: a type of sleigh with elegant curved runners.

dashboard: raised protective board in front of the driving seat.

dickey: a seat for grooms at the back of a carriage. Sometimes called a rumble.

dish: type of wheel having spokes set into the hub at an angle to give a concave appearance.

drag: a type of brake shoe. Also a term for a private coach.

dutch collar: another name for a breast collar.

evener: American term for a swingletree.

felloes: sections of the wheel rim into which the spokes are fitted.

footboard: raised board at the front of a driving seat to support the feet.

futchel: wooden or metal arm projecting from the forecarriage of a vehicle to which the shaft or splinter bar is attached.

head: a roof or hood on a vehicle.

hitch: in America a generic term for any turnout.

imperial: a luggage box carried on the roof of a travelling carriage or coach.

indispension unit: a modern form of suspension in which each wheel is individually attached to the vehicle body by an angled arm culminating in a square steel spindle set into a box lined with high-density rubber. Jolting from the wheels is absorbed by the spindle turning against the rubber lining.

kay collar: a type of full collar having the lining attached to the forewale so that no rim is visible on the inside. Also called a Prince's Forewale collar.

ladder: a folding ladder used for gaining access to the roof of a coach. Road coach ladders were made of wood; those for drags were usually iron. Also a wooden rack attached to the front or back of a harvest cart to support an overhanging load.

leaf springs: springs made up from flat, curved plates of tempered steel.

mews: originally a place where hawks were mewed (kept) but later a combined coach house and stables.

naff: term used in some parts of England for a wheel hub.

nave: another term for a wheel hub.

opera board: a protective board built into the back of some carriages to prevent the pole end of another vehicle bursting through the rear panel in the event of another vehicle running into the back.

perch: the longitudinal bar between the front and rear axles of some vehicles around which the undercarriage was built.

pin: the centre position when three horses were driven abreast.

random: three horses driven one in front of the other.

rig: American term for a complete turnout or a vehicle on its own.

roller bolt: attachment on a splinter bar to which the trace is fixed.

rumble: a seat for grooms at the back of a carriage.

skid pan: metal shoe used under the nearside rear wheel of a heavy four-wheeled vehicle to act as a crude brake.

span: an eight-in-hand team.

splinter bar: crossbeam on the forecarriage of a four-wheeled vehicle to which the shafts, pole or swingletree may be fitted.

swingletree: horizontal bar to which traces are attached on some types of vehicle.

tandem: two horses driven one in front of the other.

trandem: three horses driven abreast using two poles.

unicorn: a team composed of two wheelers and one leader. Also called a spike or pickaxe team.

whiffle tree: a swingletree between the shafts of a two-wheeled vehicle.

yard of tin: slang term of a coach horn.

Suppliers and craft firms

James Asbridge (Greenwich) Limited, 60 Banning Street, London SE10. (Coach builders and coach painters.)

Bridleways of Guildford Ltd, Smithbrook Kilns, Rural Craft Centre, nr. Cranleigh, Surrey. (Harness makers.)

Judith Cochrane, Stoneyhills, Alnwick, Northumberland. (Coach rugs and driving aprons.)

Croford Coachbuilders Ltd, Dover Place, Ashford, Kent. (Carriage builders and wheelwrights.)

Peter Durrant, 7 Cordys Lane, Trimley St Mary, Ipswich, Suffolk. (Coach painting, lining, gilding and heraldic designs.)

Fairbourne Carriages, The Oast House, Fairbourne Mill, Harrietsham, Kent. (Carriage builder and restorer, coach painting and leatherwork; supplier of brass shaft fittings, lamps, aprons and rugs. Vehicles for sale.)

Fenix Enterprises, Saxley Hill Barn, Meath Green Lane, Horley, Surrey. (Carriage builders specializing in competition vehicles.)

Freedman Harness Ltd, 1875 Dundas Street, West Toronto, Canada. (Harness makers.)

W. & H. Gidden Ltd, 112/122 Tabernacle Street, London EC2. (Harness makers.)

Richard Gill & Sons, Brame Lane, Norwood, Harrogate, North Yorkshire. (Carriage builders and restorers. Suppliers of parts and fittings.)

A. & H. Green, 237 Forest Road, Woodhouse, Loughborough, Leicestershire. (Show, working and exercise harness made to measure.)

Gryphin Harness, Glanyrafon Est., Aberystwyth, Dyfed, Wales. (Makers of competition and exercise harness.)

Alfred Hales, Manor Road, Wales, nr. Sheffield, Yorkshire. (Carriage lamp manufacturer. Supplier of all types of carriage fittings.)

Matthew Harvey & Co. Ltd, Bath Street, Walsall, Staffordshire. (Bit makers.)

Hickory Ridge Carriage & Harness Shop, Earlesville, Virginia, USA. (Repair, restoration and sale of harness and vehicles, driving accessories supplied, driving instruction given.)

Lapp's Coach Shop, 3572 West Newport Road, Ronks, Penn., USA. (Carriage restorers. Carriage parts. Vehicles for sale.)

Keith Luxford (saddlery) Ltd, 57 High Street, Teddington, Middlesex. (Harness makers.)

Martin Auctioneers Inc., PO Box 477, Intercourse, Penn., USA. (Carriage, harness and driving accoutrement auctioneers.)

Naylors Saddlery Ltd, 472 Edenfield Road, Rochdale, Lancashire. (Suppliers of show harness, holly whips, driving bits, gloves, lamps, rein rails, whip holders and aprons.)

C.J. Nicholson, Sandy Close Farm, Sherfield English, Romsey, Hampshire. (Carriage builder.)

Nodecker Carriage & Harness, 771 Ridge Road, Webster, New York, USA. (Supplier of meadowbrook carts, harness and driving accessories.)

Robeson Saddlery Ltd, 3808 Rush-Mendon Road., PO Box 221, Mendon, New York, USA. (Harness makers.)

Smucker's Harness Shop, RD3, Narvon (Churchtown), Penn., USA. (Makers of all types of harness.)

Tedman Harness, 58 Clifden Road, Worminghall, Buckinghamshire. (Show and exercise harness makers. Also driving accoutrements.)

Thimbleby & Shorland, 31 Great Knollys Street, Reading, Berkshire. (Carriage, harness and driving accoutrement auctioneers.)

Turner-Bridgar, 21 Wallingford Road, Goring-on-Thames, Reading, Berkshire. (Harness makers).

Wagon Works, 40 Bachelor Street, West Newbury, Mass., USA. (Vehicles built and restored, carriage lamps, whips, accessories.)

Weaverton Coach Shop, 3007 Old Philadelphia Pike, Bird in Hand, Penn., USA. (Carriage restorers. Also vehicles for sale.)

The Wellington Carriage Co., Long Lane, Telford, Shropshire. (Carriage builders and restorers.)

Whiting Carriage Works, Macedon, New York, USA. (Carriage builder and restorer.)

John Willie's Saddle Room Ltd., Burley, Hampshire. (Carriage builders and harness makers.)

British Driving Society, 27 Dugard Place, Barford, Warwickshire.
American Driving Society, Box 1852 Lakeville, Connecticut, USA.

A list of the names and addresses of those people prepared to give instruction in driving may be obtained from the secretary of the British Driving Society.

Carriage museums and collections

The British Isles:
Arlington Court, near Barnstable, Devon.
Bath Carriage Museum, Circus Mews, Bath, Avon.
Bristol City Museum, Queen's Road, Bristol, Avon.
Breamore House, near Fordingbridge, Hampshire.
Dodington Carriage Museum, near Old Sodbury, Avon.
Hull Museum of Transport, 36 High Street, Kingston-on-Hull, Humberside.
Open Air Museum, Beamish Hall, Stanley, Co. Durham.
The Orangery, Hampton Court Palace (April – September inclusive only).
The Royal Mews, Buckingham Palace Road, London.
The Royal Mews, Windsor Castle, St Albans Street, Windsor, Berks.
The Science Museum, Exhibition Road, South Kensington, London.
The Transport Museum, Glasgow, Scotland.
The Transport Museum, Witham Street, Belfast, Ulster.
Tyrwhitt-Drake Museum, Maidstone, Kent.
York Mills, Aysgarth Falls, near Hawes, Yorkshire.

Austria:
Kunsthistorische Museum, Schönbrunn Palace, Vienna.

Australia:
El Bodeguera Stud, El Caballo Blanco, Wooraloo, Western Australia.

Belgium:
Musée des Carrosses, Brussels.

Canada:
Devonian Foundation, 901 10th Avenue sw, Calgary, Alberta.
Remington Collection, 339 Main Street, Cardston, Alberta.

Czechoslovakia:
Hippological Museum, Slatinany Castle.

Denmark:
4684 Holme Olstrip, Sparresholm, Sjelland, near Copenhagen.

France:
Musée des Voitures, Versailles, Paris.

Germany:
Marstall Museum, Schloss Nymphenburg, Munich.

Holland:
National Rujtuigmuseum, Rienoord, Leek, near Groningen.
Het Loo Palace, near Apeldoorn.

Isle of Man:
Manx Museum, Douglas.

Italy:
Leonardo de Vinci Museum, Milan.
Museo delle Carrozze, Palazzo Pitti, Florence.

Poland:
Carriage Museum, Lancut Castle.

Portugal:
National Coach Museum, Lisbon.

Spain:
The Royal Mews, Madrid.

Sweden:
Vagn Museum, Malmo.

Switzerland:
Museum of Transport, Lucerne.

United States of America:
Smithsonian Institution, Washington DC.
Shelburne Museum, Vermont.
Suffolk Museum, Stoney Brook, Long Island, New York.
Henry Ford Museum, Deerborn, Michigan.

USSR:
The Armoury Museum, The Kremlin, Moscow.

Select bibliography

ADAMS, W. Bridges, *English Pleasure Carriages*, 1837. Reissued Adams & Dent, 1971.

ANDERSON, R.C. and J.A., *Quicksilver, A Hundred Years of Coaching 1750-1850*. David & Charles, 1973.

BATES, Alan (compiler), *Directory of Stage Coach Services 1836*. David & Charles, 1969.

HIS GRACE THE DUKE OF BEAUFORT, *Driving* (The Badminton Library). Longman, Green & Co., 1889.

BROCKLEBANK, A. Sylvia, *The Road and the Ring*, Horse Drawn Carriages, 1975.

COPELAND, John, *Roads and Their Traffic 1750-1850*. David & Charles, 1968.

CUMING, E.D., *Coaching Days and Ways*. Hodder & Stoughton, no date.

FREELOVE, William Francis, and LANG, Jennifer, *An Assemblage of Nineteenth-Century Horses and Carriages*. Perpetua Press, 1971.

GILBEY, Sir Walter, Bart., *The Harness Horse*. Vinton & Co., 1898.

GORDON, W.J., *The Horse World of London*, 1893. Reissued J.A. Allen, 1972.

HUGGETT, Frank E., *Carriages at Eight*. Lutterworth, 1979.

HUNT, Dick, *Bygones*. Baxter, 1948.

JAMIESON, Richard, *Coaching in the North Country*. Frank Graham, 1969.

KEEGAN, Terry, *The Heavy Horse – Its Harness and Decoration*. Keegan, 1973.

KNIGHT, Capt. C. Morley, *Hints on Driving*, 1884. Reissued J.A. Allen, 1969.

LEE, Charles E., *The Horse Bus as a Vehicle*. British Railway Board, 1962.

MCCAUSLAND, Hugh, *The English Carriage*. Batchworth, 1948.

PAPE, Max, *The Art of Driving*. J.A. Allen, 1982.

PEACHAM, Henry, *Coach and Sedan*, 1636. Reprinted Haslewood Books, 1952.

PITKIN PICTORIAL GUIDES, *The Royal Mews*. 1964.

RAREY, J.S., *The Taming of Horses*. Routledge & Co., 1858.

RYDER, Tom, *On the Box Seat*. Horse Drawn Carriages, 1969.

STURT, George, *The Wheelwright's Shop*. Cambridge University Press, 1942.

TARR, Lazlo, *The History of the Carriage*. Vision Press, 1969.

TRISTRAM, W. Outram, *Coaching Days and Coaching Ways*. Macmillan, 1903.

WALROND, Sallie, *Encyclopaedia of Driving*. Horse Drawn Carriages, 1974. *A Guide to Driving Horses*. Nelson, 1971.

WATNEY, Marylian, *The Elegant Carriage*. J.A. Allen, 1961.

WATNEY, Marylian and Sanders, *Horse Power*. Hamlyn, 1975.

WHEELING, Kenneth E., *Horse Drawn Vehicles at the Shelburne Museum*. Shelburne Museum, 1974.

WILSON, Violet A., *The Coaching Era*. The Bodley Head, 1922.

Index

Figures in italic refer to pages where line illustrations appear.

Abbot Downing 33
Aldridges 50
ambulances, horse-drawn 71
Amish sect 89
apron 114
Ardennes 88
Australia 33–4, 89
axle
    origins of 13
    collinge 41
    mail-box 41
axle-tree 13

bagmen 52
balancing of vehicle 108, 131
barge horses 72
barouche 57
bell, for collar 54
Besant 34
Bianconi cars 63, 90
bits, driving 108, *104–6*
'Black Brigade' 71
'black master' 71
'Black Maria' 70
blinkers 103
body makers 44
boxseat 23
brakes (on vehicle) 43, 127
break 58
breeching, full 108
breeching, false 113
brewery dray 69
britchka 56
British Driving Society 92
Brocklebank, Miss Sylvia 111
brougham 57
Brougham, Lord 57, 63

buckboard 58
buggy 58
builder's cart 70
butcher's cart 67
Buxton bit 108, *105*

cabs 61
cabriolet 53
capecart 58
caravans, gypsy 74
carriage
    maintenance of 96
    restoration 92–3
carriage-building 44–5
carriage maker 44
carrier's cart 71
carts, early origin 13
chain horse 70
chaise 52
chariot
    Celtic 14–15
    four-wheeled 16
    racing 109
    Roman 14–15
chuck-wagon racing 110
Clarence 63
Clydesdales 88
coach
    first 20
    Concord 33
    early improvements 23
    glass windows 23, 26
    hackney 22
    safety 34, 76
    stage 23
coach-building *see* carriage-building
coach horses 49, 88

breaking and training of 98–101,
    50
cost of 38
coach painters 44
coach-painting, method 45, 93
coach parade 39
coachsmiths 44
coaching classes 119
coaching club 91
coaching revival 91
coal cart 69
Coates, Romeo 53
cock horse 70
cocking cart 53
collars 101–3, 113
    how to measure *103*
    breast 103
combined driving 121–4
concours d'élégance 121
correct turnout 114
costermongers 73
crane-neck phaeton 52
curricle 53

delivery van 66
demi-mail phaeton 54
Dickens, Charles 53
dogcart 53
dog-leg whip 96
dormeuse 56
Dottridges 71
drag 120
dray 69
dress 114
dressage
    arena *116*
    test *120*
driving bits 108
dustcart 72

elbow bit 108, *106*
Elliott, Obadiah 28
Emperor of China 41
equirotal carriages 43, 128–9

farm implements, horse-drawn 75
farriers 48
Federation Equeste Internationale
    121

fibreglass, use of 127
fire engines 70–71
fishmonger's cart 67
float 67
'fly' 65
Forders of Wolverhampton 62
fourgon 56
furniture van 68

gigs 40, 52
'gondola of London' 63
governess car 55
'growler' 63
'gypsy line' 101

Hackney horse 88
Hackney pony 88
hackney stands 22
hammercloth 23
hansom cab 61
harness
    cart *118*
    correct fit of 101–3, 108
    evolution of 12
    maintenance of 96, 98
    pair 113
    parts of *102*, 113
    single 113
    tandem 114
harness racing 89, 110
hearse 71
hermaphrodite wagon 74
highflyers 51
highwaymen 16, 77
Hobson, Thomas 19
horse ambulance 73
horse copers and dealers 48
Horse and Driver's Aid Committee
    87
horse-drawn horsebox 73
horseless carriages 136

ice-cream cart 68
imperial 60

jarvey 63
jaunting car 63
jinker 58
jobmaster 47

kingpin 43, 134
knacker's cart 73

lamps 36, 93, *94*, 98, 114
lancewood 43
landau 56
landaulette 64
laundry van 68
litter, horse 17
Liverpool driving bit 108, *104*
living vans 74
'London cob' 88
long-reining 99
Lonsdale, Earl of 62, 139
Lonsdale wagonette 57
lunging 99

mail guards 37
mail phaeton 54
maintenance
    carriages 96
    harness 96, 98
marathons 115, 123
market cart 68
McAdam, John 30
Metcalfe, John 30
milk deliveries 67
modesty boards 64
Moore, Judge 111
Morgan horse 88

Norfolk Trotter 88
nosebag 119

obstacle driving 123
omnibuses
    garden-seat 64
    knifeboard 64
    private 65
'outside car' 63

Palmer, John 32
parasol whip 54
patent road protector 27
phaetons 51
    crane-neck 52
    demi-mail 54
    George IV 54
    mail 54

spider 54
    Stanhope 54
pit ponies 74, 84
ploughing 124
Pompeii 14
pony phaeton 54
Portland wagonette 57
postboys 32
post chaise 55, 60
postillion 25, 60
Post Office 32
Post Office vans 69
presentation 121
private driving 111, 115
proprietors, coaching 37
Purcell & Co. 63
putting to 100–101

racing coaches 79
railway carts 72
ralli car 55
Rarey, J. S. 98, 100
rear lamp *94*
regimental coach 121
reins, correct method of holding *107*,
    108
reinsmanship classes 118
restoration
    carriages 92–3
    harness 93
    lamps 93
ride-and-drive competitions 117
roads, Roman 15
road legislation
    Highways Act of 1555 18
    Winchester Statutes of 1285 17
road cart 58
road marathon 115
Royal Society for the Prevention of
    Cruelty to Animals 63
Rymills 50

'safety' coaches 34, 76
scurry driving 117
Selby, James 111
Shillibeer, George 64
Shire horse 88
shoeblacks 87
showman's wagon 73

Shrewsbury, Lord 63, 139
skidpans 42
skijoering 110
sledge 11
sleighs 58, 110
slide car 11
South Africa 34
spares 114
spider phaeton 54
springs
   cee 28, *29*
   dennett 42, *42*
   elliptic 28, *30*
   lancewood 43–4
   Morgan 42
   semi-elliptic 42, *42*
   telegraph 28
   whip 28, *29*
springs, early origins 23
Standard Bred horses 110
storage of vehicles 96
suicide gig 52
Suffolk Punch 88
sulky 110

T-cart 54
tandem bars 114
tanker, horse-drawn 72
Tattersalls 46, 85
Telford, Thomas 30
'tiger' 53–4
Tilbury tugs 108
Tilling, Thomas 47, 48
timber bob 75
timber for carriage construction 43
toll bridges 18
toll roads 26–7
tonga 58
town coaches 51
trade turnout 119
trams, horse-drawn 61, 65
transporting a turnout 115
travelling chariot 55–6
travelling menagerie 73
travelling wagons 74
trimmers 44
tub trap 55
tumbler cart 72
Turnpike Act 26

Turnpike Trusts 26–7
Turpin, Dick 77
tyres
   leather 14
   pneumatic 68, 87
   rubber 42
   studded 16

umbrella baskets 114
upholstery, colour of 114

Vanderbilt, Alfred G. 111
vanner 73
vehicles, colour of 114
'vestry' horse 72
veterinary remedies 49
victoria 56
Vidler of Millbank 34

wagons
   covered 16
   farm 74
   stage 19
wagons, evolution of 16
wagonette 57
wagonette-break 58
wain 74
Wells Fargo Co. 33
wheel, invention of 13
wheel, types of
   artillery or wedge 127
   dished 126
   early spoked 14
   metal 126
   tripartite 13
   warner 127
wheelwrights, early 16
whips 95–6, *95*, 98
whip, correct method of use 108
whisky 53
Wilson snaffle *104*, 108

'yellow bounder' 60
Yorkshire Coach Horse 88

zebra 34, 98, 137
zebroid 137
Zeedenburg Brothers 34